Door to Heaven

Door to Heaven

Astha Dixit

Published by Zorba Books, September 2022
Website: www.zorbabooks.com
Email: info@zorbabooks.com

Website: www.yourstrulyastha.com, www.asthadance.com
Email: info@asthadance.com
Title:- Door to Heaven

Printbook ISBN :- 978-93-93029-47-8
Ebook ISBN :- 978-93-93029-95-9

Zorba Books Pvt. Ltd. (opc)
Sushant Arcade,
Next to Courtyard Marriot,
Sushant Lok 1, Gurgaon – 122009, India

Printed by Thomson Press (India) Ltd.
B-315, Okhla Industrial Area, Phase 1, New Delhi- 110020

"I dedicate this book to all readers that have walked similarly and may have had such experiences as well as to all those that have been a part of my journey."

"If we let go of our burdens, we take a flight as a light-being towards the open sky."

Contents

Acknowledgements .... *ix*
Foreword .... *xi*
Preface .... *xiii*

Section 1

The Introduction 2
Early Memories of India 6
House on Milne Drive 10
The UCLA Experience 15
Let's Backpack Europe 22
Corporate Transition 34

Section 2

Breaking into Movies 46
Marriage and Isha 52
Sannyas Initiation 63
Passage to Braj 71
Life as a Disciple 77

Section 3

Kathak – Art of Storytelling...88
Expression of My Soul...98
Lucknow and Sufi Influence...107
Badshah's Kohi-'Noor'...116
Journey to the Middle East...125

Section 4

Dadi and My Dance Studio...140
Continuing My Spiritual Growth...153
The Breakthrough..159
In Search of Love: A Musical Production...........................165
Friends and Touring in America...174
Back to Cali...179
Journey from Beyond..185

Acknowledgements

I would like to thank my family for their support while I was working on this book. I want to acknowledge my editor, Anoo Chatrath, for being an intrinsic part of my journey in penning down my memoirs and guiding me to make this project an interesting read. Finally I want to thank Zorba Books for designing an eye-catching book cover.

Foreword

It is a great pleasure and honor for me to write the foreword for this book by Astha Dixit Joshi. I have known Astha literally from the moment she was born since I was the one who stayed with her mother in the hospital when she came into this world. It is fascinating to see her journey and where her young life has led her so far. Compared to my life—which seems straight as a road—Astha's life has been like a meandering river or perhaps better described as a range of hills, with many ups and downs. She has sought and followed many paths in search of fulfilment and happiness. But the one thing she has always stayed true to and never abandoned even for a minute is her passion and commitment to being a dancer. My earliest memories of Astha are seeing her dancing in front of a mirror, even as a little girl. Most of us outgrow our childhood hobbies but for Astha, dance was never a hobby—it was her life. It has seen her through ups and downs in her life and through some of the darkest times. This book is a frank account of Astha's life, which she has chosen to live on her terms. Throughout her life, Astha has been moving back and forth between India and the US, searching for a feeling of belonging. The moves have been disruptive at times and beneficial at others. There is a sense of belonging in both—and neither. Many young people will relate to her journey. She has written this book for them, hoping they will be inspired by her passion and commitment and her struggles to follow her dreams while overcoming all the challenges along the way. I wish this book a huge success and hope that Astha's life will continue to inspire and energize many readers.

Nisha Agrawal, Former CEO of Oxfam India

Preface

Somehow my life has taken me to the rarest and sometimes the farthest shores. In the process of self-discovery, searching for my identity and not seeming to fit in, I looked at one creative art form to fulfill my life's desires.

While most people were looking for jobs and settling down with their families, I went in the opposite direction shortly after college. I was interested in dance and movies and spent the next 15 years of my life as a stage performer with stints in mainstream cinema. I learned from a short marriage which ended in a quick divorce, and after that, I was in no rush to get married again.

I learnt that time is precious and we should follow our passions first. I was raised in Los Angeles, California, also known as the city of dreams. I enjoyed my years as a typical teenager with my friends in school. After college, I went backpacking and explored life and its wonders. *I left a lucrative IT job and moved to India to pursue my passion for dancing and acting.*

For people waiting to hit the jackpot in life, following your passion with hard work will help you earn the recognition you deserve. *I found happiness and inner contentment from the treasures that lay within me – these treasures were a result of my search and devotion to my art.*

As I sat down to write this book, the first question that came to my mind was, *'why would someone read my story?'* Immediately lots of thoughts came pouring in. Would it be for the glittery performances or challenges of a successful career in dance and film? For a first-hand experience of life after a successful career. What led me to explore places of spirituality and ashrams after my entertainment career? I share all this and more from a close perspective. By now, I have gone through so much in life that one book is not enough to summarize all of my experiences.

I narrate my life's story to the reader to share the journey of a seeker. A seeker who searched for the meaning of life through her art form – her dance – using each subtle and graceful movement to go deeper. I kept finding ways to fulfill my inner journey until, ultimately, locked within the four walls of my mind, I had to question myself. In that confinement where there was no escape, I had to find answers. I had to face my deepest fears. I overcame my own demons and emerged from that ordeal unbroken.

The journey towards self-realization comes through awareness of the self and understanding of the reality we exist in. My dance, being a vehicle for the divine or an expression of love, became my purest action or deed that ultimately transformed my life into effortless living, leading to moments of pure joy, pure bliss…

This book may be relevant for those who have been forced to face isolation, both physical and mental, only because they could not 'fit in' a normal way of life. I hope these clues to the events of my life as described here will inspire you to read this book till the end.

For the sake of privacy, I have chosen to use some fictitious names to conceal the identities of my friends and family. The definitions of the rich Kathak terminology have been interwoven in the text in the first mention for booklovers to follow. If readers pay close attention, they will also reap the benefits of learning from India's rich heritage and diverse culture.

Astha Dixit-Joshi

Section 1

The Introduction

I am standing on stage with thousands of eyes looking at me as the lights come on. I am dressed in my multi-coloured outfit adorned with flashy Indian jewellery. My heart is pounding as I take my hands up in the air... The sound of ankle bells fills the auditorium. The audience applauds as I stand still on the floor of the stage in my finale pose. The lights dim as the curtains come down in front of me. I run backstage to change for the next segment.

Those moments define the momentum of my life as a dancer. It is like an entire lifetime that continues beyond just the end of a dance. I think about my life and what brought me to the stage… Does anyone ever really know the *real* backstage story of the life of an artist? Here is the story of my life.

I was twenty-three when I went through what is called a quarter-life crisis. That would probably raise the question: why would someone just starting out in life have a crisis? My friends who were going through something similar, explained it in this way, “At our age we have so many options to choose from. We are confused.”

I asked myself why I was not happy. Upon deeper introspection I remembered what a life coach had suggested: “Decide what’s important to you. Use your personal power to follow through and begin to change the quality of your life.”

Who am I? What do I want? Am I really headed in the right direction? I repeatedly asked myself those three questions. Something struck me. It was about my identity. I wanted to know more about my roots and my cultural heritage. I lived in West Hollywood, Los Angeles from the year 2003. My family had recently moved back to India, and that raised a curiosity in me. On my next visit to India to see my parents, I did something that was different from my regular activities.

Indian cinema and music had always had a great influence on me. And I had an interest in modelling. So when a family member insisted, I got my modelling portfolio made through a talent agency in New Delhi. After spending two months relaxing with my parents, I returned to Los Angeles and my dance studio. Dance had been my greatest passion since childhood and I had recently opened my own dance company after leaving my lucrative corporate job at Deloitte. I spent a couple of months building the company website and attending rehearsals at my studio. And then, one day, I received a phone call from the same talent agency. They offered me an assignment in India.

“Hello. How are you Ma’am?” came the voice from the other end of the line. “This is the talent agency.” I heard them out. We went back and forth through a series of questions and clarifications on that first call. It was a movie – they wanted me to star in a movie! Was I really going to leave my life in Los Angeles and jump into an industry that I knew nothing about? South Indian cinema! I called them back: "Can you give me two days to think it over?"

I went back to my soul-searching. Was I truly living my life or was I living someone else's dream? Would I be able to survive in India? Was I, Astha Singhal, ready to go back to my roots, my parents and my culture? After all, *that* was my real personal identity? I was going to have to answer those questions for myself and with total honesty. Somewhere, to be very honest, I was starting to feel like a fish out of water. I loved the appreciation I received from audiences for my dance. The added movie industry glamour would be a bonus, I thought. It was a big step.

"How are you doing?" asked my friend from New York who had introduced me to the talks of the life coach. "Just fine," I told her. I had reached some sort of decision the day after the call from the agency, but I was still nervous.

I called my friend, Isaah, in Los Angeles. "At this stage you should not be confused about your life," was his advice to me. I spent another night going back and forth in my mind. The next day, Isaah called and asked me to meet him at his house that evening. Something changed in me after that meeting and I experienced a spiritual awakening. *I shut one door of my life and headed in a new direction.* That is dealt with in detail in this book.

The next morning I thought I felt something in the air. It reminded me of the sweet smell of wet mud during the rains in India. I made a call to my mother. "Mom, I'm moving to India." After the initial surprise, she was very excited. I am sure she was amazed at my own quick decision. Then I called the agency. They were thrilled.

But, before I go any further, I would like to take the reader over my life in India and the United States up until that point, and why, on the surface, everything seemed perfect, but deep down…

Life has taught me countless lessons along the way that are a part of my story. **Look out for the text that stands out in bold.** Most importantly, **I have learnt to be humble, to be grounded, and not to take anything for granted.**

Read on for the full story…

Early Memories of India

I was three years old when I started dancing non-stop around the house. Our favourite show of movie songs, *Chitrahaar*, would air on television on Sundays, and I would dance in front of the television set, emulating the actors on screen.

When I turned four, my mother called an instructor home to teach me Kathak, an Indian classical dance form. At school, I participated in all the dance competitions as well as the annual function. My family albums are full of photographs of me standing on stage in my school productions, dressed in traditional Indian outfits – the *sari, lehenga* and *salwar kameez*.

I was very naughty. I remember once climbing up on the kitchen counter at home and eating all the raw, cut cabbage kept in preparation for the evening meal. I loved spending time in front of my mother's dresser and rummaging through her drawers. "Astha! Have you taken my lipstick?"

I scored top ranks in lower elementary school, and being an obedient and disciplined student, I was a favourite of my teachers. I took my academic and curricular activities seriously and was extremely sensitive regarding my performance in both those areas of my life. I remember being scolded once in front of my entire class. It was during a school musical performance in which I had the responsibility of leading the whole group. Someone distracted me and I did not hear the teacher when she called my name. I felt humiliated. At home that evening, I cried and told my parents that I wanted to change my school. My mother met my teacher to explain what had actually happened. The air was cleared and I was my usual self again.

My maternal grandfather, who I never met but refer to as 'Nanaji', was given the title of 'Rai Bahadur' by the British during the latter's rule in India. He was gifted a one-acre estate on Hailey Road in the heart of Lutyens' Delhi near Connaught Place. My mother, the youngest of eight children, grew up in that large house along with her siblings. They had an abundant lifestyle, and there were maids and other domestic help to take care of the children and the household work. My mother, being very close to her family, visited her maternal home regularly on weekends after she was married.

I remember running around in the garden with my cousins and swinging on a *jhoola* – a rope swing, hung from a fruit tree. Mealtimes were rather lavish, and I would wait for the attendants to serve the delicacies from the kitchen. I have a special memory of my eldest cousin sister. She would dress me up in her long scarves called *dupattas*, to resemble saris, and often made designs with henna on my palms. I loved it and can never forget how it felt to have an older sister like her.

Life in India was not easy for my father. He was a chartered accountant and in the 1980s there was limited scope, after a certain point, for growth in his profession. He wanted a better life for his family. As his elder brother lived in Los Angeles in California, my father applied for a green card to the United States. After a long wait of seven years, he received a letter from the American embassy calling him for his interview. His dream of moving to America finally came true.

Having a large, close-knit family in India and that too with most of our relatives living in New Delhi and the neighbouring areas, made it hard to say goodbye. As we hugged and kissed at the airport, I turned back one last time to look at my cousins, aunts and uncles. I was only eight and still in elementary school.

We arrived at the Los Angeles International Airport, or LAX as it is called, and were received by my uncle. To begin with, we were to live at his house in the southwestern region of Los Angeles, by the coast in an area called Torrance. Carrying our own luggage up the front porch into this large two-storied house with wall-to-wall carpeting felt very new.

I started school in the middle of the academic year. Completely new to the American culture, I remember how, initially, I had a tough time. I felt strange seeing everyone dressed in casual jeans and T-shirts as there was no school uniform. I had to wear the frocks I had brought from India and was made fun of for wearing those. I had to adjust my attire fast. To add to it, I was looked at strangely by some students because of my accent.

After school, I spent my evenings with my brother playing board games well into the night. The next morning I would dread going to school and facing all the bullies around. I once cried to my mother, “Why are we here? Let’s go back to India.” I would think of the smiling faces of my cousins back home and remember the fun we had. In those days I found it very difficult to stay half-way across the world.

The move came with a big adjustment for my parents as well. My father filled his time by managing a small newspaper company while he studied for his Certified Public Accountant (CPA) examination. After passing the examination, he got a job as a finance manager in a firm.

We shifted to a rented apartment that had two bedrooms. The complex had a swimming pool and tennis courts. My next-door neighbour would invite me to her house to play with her Barbie dolls. I also started playing tennis with another neighbour who was a good athlete.

I met Renu at the local community event held on Sundays called Bal Vihar where Indian children were taught to speak Hindi. I was already good at the language and so would help the teachers teach the other children. After class we would play cricket and kho-kho, a traditional Indian sport, in the fields outside. Our parents did not want us to lose touch with the Indian culture, so Bal Vihar was their initiative to keep us connected to it.

Three years after our arrival in the States, my parents bought their own house on Milne Drive. It turned out to be only a few blocks from where Renu lived with her family. Slowly, she and I became good friends.

House on Milne Drive

The house on Milne Drive was where I spent my formative years in the United States. Many of my childhood memories are attached to it. It was located at the corner of a *cul-de-sac* so it was a safe neighborhood in South Bay, Torrance. The house had a tall Christmas tree, as we called it. A variety of fir, it stood in the front of the house and was beautiful. Right behind the house was the playground of the elementary school that my brother went to. I joined middle school. My school was located down the road, a short distance from home. Renu too went there.

Renu and I formed a group called NARS along with two of our best friends. The first letter of each of our names spelt NARS. We were: Nina, Astha, Renu and Shivani. Our mothers had us join a Kathak dance class that we attended together after school. The four of us lived within a ten-kilometre radius of one another, and as we met regularly, our families became a tight-knit group.

Poonam Kumar, our Kathak teacher of fine repute, lived and taught in South Bay. Seeing my enthusiasm for dance, she began giving me special attention. *Ta a thei e i tat…* The call of her Kathak notations reminded me of my *ghungroos* as a little girl – I would love to wear the musical anklet worn by Indian classical dancers and dance around the house to the sound of the little bells. I began taking part in the events of the Vishwa Hindu Parishad, a Hindu organization run by Shivani's father.

"NARS, please come to the dining table," came my mother's voice, trying to calm us rowdy girls. As is typical of teenage life, during those years we would be on the phone with one another for hours, and our mothers would chide us for talking so much. I remember my fourteenth birthday. We invited all our friends to our house. When my mother broke the piñata in the air, how we ran around screaming and pushing each other, trying to pick the toys and sweets up from the floor.

I entered high school. Renu and I would meet during our lunch break to exchange letters. We had crushes on Bollywood movie stars such as Akshay Kumar and Salman Khan for whom we kept nicknames. Our letters to each other went something like this: "Dear Akki, I couldn't pay attention in class today. The teacher was talking on and on about something..." Our antics went unnoticed for a long time until our class teacher caught us passing letters. We were given detention.

Once we decided to hold a fashion show in my house. We got my brother to set up the camera and Renu's brother to read the script out loud. "The next theme is, 'The girl next door,'" read Renu's brother as we posed in casual outfits. Then we lined up as beauty queens, and in the finale, we had the 'Bollywood fashion' theme where we wore our mothers' Indian attire.

One day, the four of us sneaked out to meet our boyfriends at a movie theatre in the neighbourhood. As we stood in the line to get in, Shivani's father happened to pass by. He told our parents. They held a meeting and decided amongst themselves that we, NARS, would not meet or talk to one another for a whole month.

Best Friends Growing Up

When I turned sixteen, I became conscious of my attractive looks. I also knew how to get my way with my friends. My friends and I enjoyed visiting nightclubs. My parents were at peace knowing that my entire gang was together and that as long as we stayed together in a group we were safe.

Boys would approach us and after a mocktail at the bar we would get on the dance floor. We would take turns in the centre, moving our waists to the beat of the music.

I started taking part in the Ziba Dance Competition, an annual contest for the youth in Los Angeles. I was third runner-up in the first year. The following year I went on stage with a unique prop – a five feet, seven-inch frame that my father designed for the event. It gave the effect of me coming alive when the music began. I took the first prize home that year.

Around the same time, I participated in the Miss LA India beauty pageant (1996). I remember being extremely nervous in front of the judges. In the first round I walked in a beautiful backless silver dress, and for the Indian segment, I wore a blue sequinned *sharara*. But what got the attention of the judges was my dance to the evergreen Hindi movie song, "Inhi logon ne…" wearing a traditional stone-embellished Anarkali suit to complete the look of the actress in the movie. I ended with a Kathak expression and spin. I scored the highest in the talent segment and won Second runner-up in the pageant. I got nervous in the question-answer round and missed the title. Both *sharara* and *Anarkali* come from the Mughal influence in India and are now an essential part of the traditional outfits worn in the country.

My high school prom dance, that being my first prom in the United States, was just around the corner. I chose a well-built, handsome Latin-American boy as my dance date, and we decided to go along with another couple from school in their car. On the way we, my date and I, sat in the back seat. He tried to hold my hand; I brushed his hand away. He repeatedly tried to touch me and I got annoyed. When we arrived at the venue of the gala, I left him and went on my own to the dance floor. I forgot about him and enjoyed dancing by myself in my favourite backless silver dress. At the end of the evening, in spite of my having ignored him the whole time, he had the guts to ask me if I would go to a hotel with him. I flatly refused.

When high school ended we, NARS, went our separate ways. The youngest one stayed back in school; one went to a different college; and Nina and I moved into the dormitory housing at UCLA – the well-known University of California, Los Angeles, on the West Coast.

The same time that I commenced my first year of college, my parents moved from Torrance to Irvine, a city in Orange County. I would visit home on the weekends.

Many times when I entered the house, my mother would be cooking in the kitchen. The air would be filled with the aroma of Indian spices. My father, who had stepped up to higher posts, was by then the vice president of his company. He would be home late from work and we would sit around the dining table in the kitchen that overlooked the patio in the back garden. When dinner was over, we would pick up our plates and then leave my mother to finish the cleaning. I would go up to my room and read or just sit by the window overlooking the street below to watch the night lights filter through the green foliage of the line of trees.

I know those years of my childhood, the innocence and the fun times, will never come back. Nonetheless, I have held on to my playfulness. As Osho-Rajneesh once said, "The freshness of the child is the freshness of your consciousness, which never becomes old, which always remains young."

My takeaway from that time was: **"Grow up but not old and maintain your innocence. And allow friendships to bloom and take on their own fragrance – when it is time, allow yourselves to go your ways."**

The UCLA Experience

My freshman year at UCLA was, as expected, challenging. I had scored the highest in my Advanced Placement subjects in high school and had to immediately start my computer programming courses as a part of my College of Engineering computer science degree at UCLA. I learnt many computer programming skills during my undergraduate studies including software, hardware and operating systems. I would go home on the weekends to get my mind off the difficulty of the studies and to bring some of my mother's home-cooked food back with me.

My best friend Nina and I stayed in a dormitory together. We often walked back and forth between our classes on campus and our dormitory. I remember walking uphill for hours to get to our dormitory building and stopping on the way to eat at the dining hall. My studies throughout the first and second years were very hard and I often stayed up late in the night, cramming all the formulas for my midterm examinations. It was a tough degree, one with a very high boy-to-girl ratio.

Other than my studies, during the four years, I met some interesting people some of whom I ended up sharing off-campus housing apartments with. We had some engaging conversations about college and life in general as we used to stay up late at night studying or hanging out.

I remember one time when we were in the study hall. Nina asked, "So what are you guys planning on doing after graduation?" She had a twinkle in her eyes as she looked up from her big, thick biology book. "Most of us are planning on finding our soulmates, right?" she said, "then we can get a job in a reputable company, get married, settle down and have a family. What do you'll think?" I was trying to focus on writing my new recursive equation but nearly lost it and put my pen down. Next thing, I was thinking of my family and what that family would consist of. I could picture at least two loud, wild kids running around a cozy home... messy floors with toys littered everywhere… and the curled-up family pup looking at us humans and thinking that we must be crazy and from another planet! Thanks to my best friend, the late nights were a lot more fun because of those conversations.

For most Indian children who have grown up in Indian families with Indian values, we maintain and uphold certain values with the pride and privilege of our culture. The *sindoor* – the orange-red coloured cosmetic powder from the Indian subcontinent that a married woman wears on her forehead – signifies wedlock and a certain feeling of pride of belonging to her new family. I grew up cherishing dreams of being married and having my own family one day. Vivid images of a bridal-coloured sari would flash through my mind. I was excited to finally finish college and move on.

After graduation, my friends and I went our ways. I scored one of the highest ranks academically – Magna Cum Laude – at UCLA and found my dream job. I had offers from various leading technology and consulting companies. I chose Deloitte Consulting (Deloitte & Touche being one of the big five audit and consulting firms) because its head office in Orange County was close to my parents' house. However, I told the HR manager of the firm that I would not join office right away. I wanted three months off. After I had barely survived the four years of computer engineering, I first wanted to enjoy the real world.

My lesson from UCLA was: **"Go for your goal. There are infinite ways to succeed. Those who strive for something greater than themselves eventually stand out from the crowd."**

Summer Internship in New York

After my first year of college, I did an internship with Scient Corporation in New York City. That was at the height of the dot-com boom, and I had applied for the placement earlier during my academic year. In 1998, it was one of the most sought-after summer programmes. Scient was an information technology company based out of San Francisco with offices in New York, London and Paris. My office was at Union Square, in the financial district in lower Manhattan. The elevator took us to the fifth floor of an old, converted Andy Warhol building. Andy Warhol, an American artist and a leading figure in the visual art movement, was a movie producer and director. The building had been his studio and gave the feeling of a warehouse.

On my first day when I walked into the office, I was pleasantly surprised by the culture that prevailed in those dot-com days. Exposed electric wiring came through the ceiling and down poles to desks furnished with the latest equipment, desktop computers and laptops. Everyone sat in their open cubicles talking on their phones. The energy in the office looked like the trading floor of a stock market or even a warehouse party, very much in keeping with the software engineering culture of that time.

As I sat at my desk, my eyes caught a tall fair boy walking into the pantry. I walked across to get my coffee. He smiled at me and we started chatting. "You're new here, aren't you?" he asked. My heart began doing a funny dance under my new collared top.

Next day, in the evening, he and I visited a dimly-lit cafe called Milk and Honey in the underground district of Chelsea. He was my tour-guide into the underground scene of New York. Then he took me out to the Manhattan Bridge from where we could see the entire city: its lights and cars whizzing by. Lastly, we went to a night club. We danced all night. After he took me back to my apartment, I hesitated to take the relationship any further. I told him that I would call him the next day.

That time spent at Scient was unexpected – it was everything imaginable all at once. The summer flew by and before I knew it I was headed back to Los Angeles.

That summer internship taught me: **"It is not others who hold you back; it is always YOU who holds yourself back."**

A Vacation in Miami

After my second year at UCLA, some of us friends planned a weekend in Miami together. It was an all-girls group – Renu and her friend Kaley came from Cornell; Indira from New York; and Nina, along with a friend, flew down from Canada. We rented a house on Ocean Drive next to the crystal blue waters. Bimal, a friend from UCLA, along with his group, also landed up. They rented a house just a street down from our accommodation. South Beach was the hangout place during that spring break. In the mornings we would take long walks along the famous Ocean Drive, and in the evenings, enjoy going to restaurants and malls. At night we visited the nightclubs.

In the gang of friends that Bimal brought, there was an interesting personality named Dunster. He had the habit of disappearing in the middle of the night while we bought our drinks. We would find him the next morning, by himself, outside some nightclub. An incident comes to mind that happened in the beginning of our vacation.

One morning, we decided to take jet skis out into the ocean. Kaley had decided to go separately with her boyfriend. Some of the others were already in the water. I looked around for a partner but, suddenly, could not see anyone. Only Dunster was left. I was afraid. "After last night's party, he should be sober enough by now…" I thought to myself. He looked at me with an open smile, "Wanna go together?" "Um... yeah, sure," I replied. We hit the waves on our newly-rented Kawasaki.

Out in the middle of the ocean we did a turnaround with the jet ski and came back towards the coastline. Just as we were about to hit the shore, Dunster did a complete three-hundred-sixty-degree turn and the waves toppled us over.

I looked at him. "Where is the jet ski?" I yelled, trying not to swallow water as the waves came above our heads. "I dunno..." he said casually. I tried to stay calm. "Over there," he pointed out. I saw it in the distance floating on its side. We both swam towards it and as he climbed back on the driver's seat, he took my hand and helped me up.

I was just starting to get comfortable in the blue waters of Miami Beach and was enjoying the Sun's rays on me when he asked, "You wanna ride now?" "Ok," I said. I took the wheel. We took full turns around in the water. "I have an idea," he said. I looked at him. "Ok, what?" "You sit right where you are and I'll ride the jet ski from the back." I did not quite understand what he was saying but went along. Dunster took the wheel from behind me and, before I knew it, we were racing into the wind. He suddenly turned the handle so hard, our bodies were flung in the air and the weight of the jet ski landed on my foot.

That was only the second day of our vacation. We got into a taxi and drove to a nearby hospital. That night I could not carry my crutches into a nightclub so my friends carried me on their shoulders. I will never forget the expression on the bouncer's face as we went inside.

Our nights were colorful, vivid and full of curiosity and entertainment. Irrespective of my swollen foot, I danced that night away. *The music was so loud around me that I could not hear anyone talking, but I could certainly feel the rhythm in my body.* One thing I remember fondly is, on our way into the nightclub, as we were passing through multiple brightly-lit hallways, Kaley looked at me and whispered something in my ear. I think I heard the line, "The party must go on!"

South Beach was a happening place throughout the day and night. It had a fun vacation culture, one that neither my gang nor Bimal's will ever forget. One more moment that I remember is Nina's expression when Dunster and I came out of the water after the jet ski incident. "Next time, maybe you can ride in a straight line?" Her comment came across as a lesson.

The lesson: **Take a straight path in life when you want to enjoy the ride.**

A note about my friendships: I loved to have reunions with my college friends and the people that I grew up with. We generally went to private parties or nightclubs and enjoyed our moments of camaraderie. Every few years we re-evaluated where we stood in our life-goals and discussed our achievements with each other. The reunions became a sort of measuring scale to gauge our progress in where we stood in life regarding our partners, careers, jobs and families.

So, besides being a great measure for your life, "your friends are your peers and they are there for you to enjoy the ride of life with!"

Let's Backpack Europe

I took three months off before starting my first job. After graduation, some of my engineering friends planned to travel Europe during the summer and they convinced me that it was something worth experiencing. I was excited and decided to join them.

I had a backpack filled with my clothes and essentials along with a smaller backpack to take on daily sightseeing tours. "Are you going to be able to take that around with you?" asked my mother, as she saw me lifting the weight of the entire thing on my back. "Don't worry," I said. I was pretty confident. I had tried my best to pack as light as possible but somehow the size of my backpack did not reflect it. In my backpack I had a paperback edition of the *Let's Go Europe* travel guide.

I have always felt there are benefits to the culture of backpacking in Europe. Backpackers can choose affordable accommodation from a mix of options. There are youth hostels, dormitories and single rooms that are neat and clean, and the staff is friendly. Moreover, backpackers get to meet with the most exciting of people that are in Europe at the time. Yet another advantage is they get exposed to the culture of each country from up close – the accommodations being located very much in the heart of the countries.

I flew into London and then took a flight to Berlin to meet my friends. Each one of us was on a budget for the summer. We had customized our itinerary so we could take advantage of the summer festivals along the way. All set with our Eurail Passes in our wallets and our travel guides, the four of us were ready to explore Europe. In our first circuit we visited Berlin, Rome, Florence and Prague.

Circuit One

Berlin, known for its *biergartens* or beer gardens, and nightlife, was more advanced than I had read about in German history. The cars there flew by at faster speeds than in any of the neighboring countries. We looked outside our train. Being engineering students, we took turns measuring the distance against the velocity of the train, trying to calculate if we would arrive at our destination on time. We did. One of my friends pointed to a place on the map, and I followed closely behind him as we made our way through the crowds with the pages of the map fluttering in the breeze.

BackpackerBerlin was a hostel with the highest occupancy rate in the summer. Yes, even hostels got sold out during peak seasons, being the cheapest accommodation for young people travelling to Europe. In fact, many times we had to call a hostel a day in advance to make our bookings. Despite our efforts we could not get a room at the BackpackerBerlin; however, we managed to get two rooms in an apartment three buildings from there.

We visited the Reichstag building on the day that we arrived in Berlin. I had seen many pictures of the historic building, yet we could not stop clicking photographs of its Renaissance architecture. We lingered on the lawn in front of the building for a long time. Right there I made a mental note that when I returned home, I would make a souvenir album of the trip to contain all my ticket stubs of the museums and other places we would be visiting as well as the photographs and mementos that I would collect.

East and West Berlin were separated by the Berlin Wall from 1961-89. We visited Checkpoint Charlie, the spot known for border crossing when the city was divided during the Cold War. It reminded me of the graffiti I had seen as a child and also the paintings of artists that expressed the plight of families who were divided and unable to visit each other. The partition had caused a lot of hardship. We stood there silently, paying homage to the people who had lost their lives while attempting to illegally cross the wall.

Our next destination was Rome. When we arrived at Beehive Hostel, another great find in our friendly Europe travel guide, we found it pleasant and welcoming. We were given our locker keys and directed to our floor in the building. We crossed over to the elevator through the game room and lounge with a small video arcade. On the way to our dormitory I heard someone speaking in a particular accent.

"Well…hello…how are ya'lll doing and what brings you to this beautiful part of Europe?" he said, drawing out the "ya...ll". He was lean and had chiselled features. I looked at him in amazement, trying to place his accent and where he was from. "Hi. I'm Ronald. I'm from Austraiiiilia." As soon as he said it, I thought excitedly about how much there is to learn in the world. We all introduced ourselves.

The same day we visited St. Peter's Basilica museum and strolled around the courtyard taking photographs. That evening, as we sat at a dining table on our terrace, Ronald the Aussie led the conversation. He told us that he was born and raised in Down Under – a term referring to Australia's location – and that his parents were originally from India. It came as no surprise to us. He had the look of an Indian. He had a great sense of humour and said things that made us laugh out loud. In fact all of us took turns telling jokes. During the meal I caught him glancing at me a few times. After everyone left to get an early night's sleep, Ronald and I were alone on the terrace. Before he could say anything I made it very clear to him that I was not interested.

The next day was spent wandering through the thick walls of the structure of the Colosseum. By the evening we were exhausted. The next morning was the Sistine Chapel. Not knowing Rome had so many sights that one could explore, we were pleasantly surprised. After a bit of a history lesson at the Sistine Chapel in the Apostolic Palace, the official residence of the pope in the holy Vatican City, we covered the sights of the Trevi Fountain and the Roman Forum.

Finally we arrived in Florence or Firenze, also known as Italy's 'capital of arts'. We took off our backpacks at the reception desk of an accommodation, and I waited by a window while my friends made the reservations. As we were going up the stairs to our room, one of the others told me that someone had invited us to a nightclub.

There was a large group of art students at the nightclub who had been in the city for the past few months doing their summer internships while on holiday, and I met all of them. From the bumping and colliding of people against me from all sides as we were dancing, all I can remember is the big smiles they carried on their faces. I stayed back in Florence for an extra week. I could not get enough of the city. I fell in love with its culture and its people. Most of all, I enjoyed sitting by myself across from the Duomo in the evenings, watching people go by. The iconic cathedral of Florence was awe-inspiring. Brunelleschi's dome of the Duomo glistened and looked even more beautiful in the evenings when there were less tourists around it.

According to *National Geographic*, "The Basilica di Santa Maria del Fiore (in English, "Cathedral of Saint Mary of the Flower"), nicknamed the Duomo after the enormous octagonal dome on its east end is, arguably, the birthplace of the Renaissance." The dome of the cathedral was completed sometime in the fifteenth century. Its curves and innovative design were striking to look at.

I caught up with my friends in the city of Prague, the capital of the Czech Republic. We spent the next day exploring the city. After our sightseeing, as we were walking back to our hotel, we stopped at a restaurant. "Next time, I'll take an appointment with the pope," said a friend in jest, still unable to forget the number of incredible things we had seen and experienced in Rome. "Yeah... he must be busy," I mumbled as I bit into my sandwich. I suddenly remembered the adage that Rome was not built in a day.

We felt we needed a break as it had been rather hectic until then and decided to extend our stay in Prague. With its tall castles and impeccably-lined streets with statues all around, it was true to its fairy-tale stories. The city was captivating and it naturally demanded more time to explore.

Soon we were ready to travel to our next destination. We had just arrived at the station and were looking up the schedule when the train we were supposed to take started moving. As we sped towards it, the train went past us and left the platform. We looked at each other. "Now what?" I said. We took our backpacks off, sat down and pulled out our itinerary.

I guess fate was telling us to experience a little more of the culture of the country we were in. We took a bus back into the city and stayed at another budget hostel for the night. **When things become chaotic, take a moment aside and allow things to flow.**

Circuit Two

Our other circuit was Barcelona, Pamplona, Amsterdam, Paris and a final quick stop in London.

I will start with Barcelona. Many tourists might narrate stories of their experiences at Las Ramblas, but they would not have quite experienced it the way that I did. In Barcelona, I met a young girl named Luna. This is how it happened. Pulling up at the train station, we carried our heavy bags to the main crossing of Las Ramblas – a wide, tree-lined street that runs through the heart of the city centre. We looked around and found the hostel that we had tried to contact a day earlier. We wanted a booking for two nights but were told there was no vacancy. We then walked up to St Christopher's Inn. In the reception area I met Luna.

She looked at me. "Ahem," she cleared her throat. "Everyone thinks we look the same." She pointed towards her friends who were smiling at us. My friends were amused at our resemblance too. I took one look at Luna's backpack and started laughing. It was uncanny! She carried one exactly like mine. And it was made of the same fabric and colour. *For me, who was looking for experiences, in that moment she was like my best friend.* I thought: fate had brought me to St Christopher's Inn. Everything happens for a reason?

She and I walked outside to the plaza near our hostel in Central Barcelona. There were children playing in the large square called Plaza de Cataluna. I was already starting to feel the vibe of the Spanish culture and was so happy that we had come to Spain. "So what do you think of Barcelona?" she asked. "I dunno," I shrugged. "I haven't seen much yet." She invited me out the next night with her friends. "Well, here's your chance. We're going to Maremagnum, the best place by the water in the city. Join us after your daytime exploring." She left me with that.

The next morning my friends and I began our sightseeing by visiting the Sagrada Família. A giant Roman Catholic basilica designed by the famous architect Antoni Gaudi, it has been under construction since 1882. It is expected to be completed by 2026 to mark the hundredth year of Gaudi's death. Although incomplete, it stands out as one of the most extraordinary designs of Gothic architecture.

In the evening I met Luna and her friends outside the hostel. Both of us wore a similar-styled outfit. We took a taxi and drove past Port Olímpic, where the sailing events of the 1992 Summer Olympics had been held, to arrive at the Maremagnum complex nightclubs located in the old port of Barcelona.

The next day, along with my college friends, I set off on foot to see the genius Gaudi's marvels. We visited the fantastic sites of the Gaudi museums in the coastal city of Barcelona that lies in the northeastern region of Spain, also known as Catalonia. At night I enjoyed the activities of the central plaza with Luna.

"The Spanish festival is starting in two days," our friend who had planned all the festivals reminded us as he made a note in his travel guide. "Ok, backpackers!" he announced, "we have to move on if we don't want to miss the bulls." "Oh no! We have to see the bulls!" another friend exclaimed. We absolutely agreed with her. Our planner began calling some phone numbers and I looked out at the street outside. The days were going by quickly and the nights were not getting longer. I made a mental note to start taking notice of the number of days left on our trip. "We're going to Pamplona, but…" our friend said, as he got off the phone. He gave us the news that there were no hotel rooms available in Pamplona. We would have to spend our entire time there under the open skies. The four of us put our heads together and decided to stay one extra night in Barcelona instead. We looked at each other. "Can we do it?" asked one, with a half-smile and a twinkle in his eyes. We gave him the thumbs up.

We arrived in Pamplona on the opening day of the festival. The availability of public bathing facilities and toilets as well as lockers provided by the government for the festival, helped us manage without accommodation. We were on foot with our daypacks and water bottles, and ready for the Spanish bulls. We did not sleep that night but roamed the city. We walked through the large crowds and went to the other side where the festival was going to be held. "The running of the bulls is tomorrow," we kept hearing people say. We spent the whole night at food stalls. We filled our stomachs with a variety of foodstuff that the locals eat, listened to music and waited for the morning of the big run.

According to the official tourism website of Spain, "The city of Pamplona is world-famous for its fiestas of San Fermín Festival. Thousands of people go there every year to experience the risk and the thrill of the running of the bulls..." The traditional festival called: The festival of San Fermín or The Running of the Bulls, attracts runners from all over the world. The event is rooted in the true spirit of the Spanish tradition and culture.

On the morning of 7 July, the first day of the run, the narrow roads and alleys were jam-packed with people dressed in white with traditional red handkerchiefs wrapped around their necks. Music blared from speakers. At 8 am, the sound of a rocket fired into the sky announced the opening of the bullpens. Then a second rocket went off, indicating that the bulls were on the streets.

People scurried inside the shelter of their homes and watched from their balconies. Tourists chose to be at different restaurants, cafes and other places that had their shutters down. We stood on the balcony of a restaurant as we looked out.

Not a person stayed on the streets who did not dare to be caught in the path of the bulls.

We saw them approaching, gigantic creatures with big horns. We watched the runners waiting on the street below us, and as the bulls came round the corner, they ran in front of them. There were many who ran beside the animals, trying to touch them. We, the onlookers, shouted and screamed madly to cheer them on. The runners knew how to dodge the bulls when the latter took wide turns on street corners. It was something to be witnessed. A third rocket indicated that the bulls had entered the Plaza de Toros, the bullring arena at the end of the run.

The crowds gathered around in the stands of the ring to watch. I saw a large number of people run into the centre of the arena, and feeling that I was safe in the presence of the matador, I too followed them into the ring. Just then I saw a bull coming towards me from a short distance. I looked around. There was no place to run from the creature, but I turned and ran for my life. I managed to jump to a side where the bull could not reach me, just as I had seen the runners do. After the bullfight someone came up and commended me for my swift action. The firing of a fourth and final rocket signalled that the streets were once again open for the festivities to continue. We went out and enjoyed ourselves while the bulls played with the matadors.

We went from Spain to Amsterdam. The Canal District, the red-light district area and the nearby posh nightclubs were at a short distance from our hostel. It was convenient for us to sightsee as well as enjoy the nightlife side of Amsterdam.

Despite the fact that we were backpacking, the journey was smooth, thanks to the meticulous planning of our very own guide, my college engineering friend. A complete Eurail package during one summer can be an intensive experience to have. It can only be done once in a lifetime. We managed to make it to almost every festival in those peak summer months of June and July, in spite of the large number of tourists. What was left? The city of Paris with its ongoing Tour de France – one of the world's most prestigious and difficult bicycle races.

The moment we landed in Paris, we felt like tourists lost in a big French city. As we were making our way to see one of the world's monumental wonders – the great, big Eiffel Tower – we saw the race riders completing their final round around the city. They passed us along the Champs-Elysees and we waved at them as they rode at breakneck speed into the distance to do a turnaround at the Eiffel Tower. It was an amazing experience to spend the entire day at the monument with my engineering buddies. We stared long at the height of the structure and took in all the details of the columns. It was just as I recollected from a thousand different photographs on the internet.

I remember an interesting encounter with a French woman while we were on our way to the Eiffel Tower in a metro train. We were confused regarding which stop to get off at. I looked at the lady sitting across from me. "Which stop is the Eiffel Tower?" I asked her. After my repetitive attempts at trying to pronounce the words 'Eiffel Tower' in every possible French way, she still had not understood me. The metro was running fast and I knew our stop was approaching. I quickly pointed to the travel guide sitting on my lap. "Ma'am, where is this monument?" "Ah... the Eiffel..." she nodded and pointed to the station outside where the train had just come to a halt. The doors opened and we quickly picked up our bags and dashed out.

I had tried to speak in French, the local language that I find fascinating and very romantic. I remembered the saying, "Never speak to a Frenchman in French." That evening we visited one of the local nightclubs near our accommodation and on the following day we went to the Louvre Museum.

It was time to take the high-speed bullet train to central London. Once there, we bade goodbye to one another with a warm hug. Nothing more needed to be said. My friends went on to take their flight back to the United States.

A short taxi ride later, I arrived at my cousins' place on the outskirts of London. I barely spoke to anyone before going to my room to doze off. I must have slept the whole night and all of the next afternoon, and the family was amazed that they hardly got to see me. I left the morning after.

The lesson: **I could have spent a year in Europe with its variety of cultures. Each culture is reflected through its people when they meet you.**

"The experience of backpacking is an adventure with
adjustment at every step.
If you flow with it, it becomes an incredible journey.

Corporate Transition

The moment I arrived back in Los Angeles from my backpacking tour, things took a different turn. It was the time of the United States recession of 2001-2002 when the internet bubble burst and there was a downturn in the economy. It affected all information technology companies, large and small, because of which Deloitte had to delay my joining date. To give an idea of the events of that time, technology companies were downsizing and some were even laying off due to the dot-com bubble bust that was associated with the stock market crash. I was eager to move on to the workforce in the corporate world, so I applied and got a job as a software engineer, commonly known as programmer, at Northrop Grumman, an American global aerospace and defense technology company.

My days were long and demanding. My first project involved working on the software upgrades to the F/A-18 Super Hornet, the US Navy's fighter aircraft. My supervisor took me along with him on field trips to the site of the wind tunnel testing where the simulated F/A-18 Hornet was taken on practice flights. On my first visit, I sat in one of those simulated control booths and began to play with the take-off device. The plane started moving and almost crashed immediately. My supervisor looked at me and laughed.

I thoroughly enjoyed the intense research and development related projects at Northrop, although my focus was more on the high-technology consulting environment where new systems are developed for clients. After a brief stint at Northrop, I had to leave when my position at Deloitte opened up. My supervisor was sad to see me leave, but he supported me in my decision to move on towards my chosen career path in business management at Deloitte.

The next week I was back in Orange County at the head office of Deloitte Consulting. It was only a fifteen-minute drive from my parents' house. I was posted to various client sites as representative of the company. While working at Deloitte, I serviced companies such as Walt Disney World, Nissan, Verizon and Hewlett Packard (HP) in the San Francisco Bay Area.

I considered my posting at HP in the bay area a big break in my career. I was given the responsibility of a functional head of a business division giving requirements to the software engineers, and I was responsible for reporting directly to the HP marketing team.

I packed my bags and headed for the headquarters in Cupertino. The area is referred to as Silicon Valley – a region in the southern part of San Francisco Bay Area in California that serves as a global centre for technology and systems innovation. Cupertino is one of its major cities.

A senior consultant from Deloitte met me outside the HP office building and introduced me to my other team members from the Deloitte office.

On the first day itself I felt at home in the office environment at the HP site. I sat at my desk and opened my email. The incoming messages reflected the new layout of the system that I was responsible for. I started working on my spreadsheet. When it was lunchtime, I joined my team and we went out for food.

Another day passed. I was amazed at how fast the days were passing. Soon the weekend arrived and it was time for me to catch my flight back to Orange County. Two weeks after my joining our client, the managers at HP were happy with my progress. They asked John, my manager, to involve me in certain important meetings. I was sent to their offices in Singapore and Tokyo to head discussions on the projects that Deloitte was upgrading at HP's marketing divisions as a consultant. The older systems no longer kept up with the company's increasing demands. I held related discussions with the leaders of the marketing divisions in Singapore and Tokyo.

During my next visit to Orange County I sat on my bed, reflecting on my trip with the HP managers and my work at Deloitte until then. The meeting in Tokyo had gone rather well, I thought, and they were satisfied with the system. However, in Singapore, the team with which I had conducted the sessions had had certain stricter requirements. I knew there was work to be done in the coming days. When I returned to Cupertino that week, I got busy incorporating the new requirements into the HP system.

The United States economy recovered slightly during my year at HP, so my team members and I started staying in San Francisco. I remember the stylish boutique hotels that we put up at in those days. Often, in the evenings, we would be at a swanky bar in downtown San Francisco for an evening out. Those were fun moments after work with my colleagues and friends in the bay area amidst the corporate environment in the US.

Back home, my parents had moved into their new house in Orange County. It was again an upgrade from the previous one with a large pool in the backyard. But, suddenly, my father got an offer from his company that had global operations in several countries to move to India. The new office was to be opened in Gurugram, a centre for technology growth in the Delhi NCR region.

When I visited my parents, they sat across the table from my brother and me and gave us the big news. We looked at them with blank expressions. We could not believe they were moving to India. In a flash, all the old memories came pouring in. I tried to block them. Three months later, in 2006, my parents bade us goodbye at LAX – the same airport that we had arrived at the first time from India. I was too stunned to realize what had just happened.

I went back to my work at Deloitte; I was well set in my role as a consultant. My parents had left but I continued to visit Los Angeles on the weekends and when placed at client work sites. I rented a studio apartment in West Hollywood perched right above Sunset Boulevard. Along with some friends, I started a dance company there and named it after a rhythmic beat pattern – 'Taal'. My dance group and I rehearsed on the weekends when I visited.

Those were some glorious days of my life living in West Hollywood and performing amidst celebrities, which included the post red-carpet event at the 58th Primetime Emmy Awards in 2006. The highlight of that period was that I had the fortune to entertain the divas of Hollywood and perform my dance skills for the likes of Ron Howard and George Lucas. My dancers and I performed at various Hollywood events with industry stalwarts including a Pepsi commercial with world renowned pop singer, Christina Aguilera. We also performed for the Bollywood celebrities who attended the opening of the Indian Film Festival of Los Angeles in 2003.

Later that year, I started to experience a dissatisfaction with where I was headed. *Something was not right.* I tried identifying what it was, but could not. I realized there had to be a reason for my unhappiness – **everything has an underlying reason. It was a quarter-life crisis that I went through. Nothing made sense.** A quarter-life crisis is generally defined as a period of insecurity and doubt about one's career, life goals or purpose, and may include relationships. I felt jaded in a corporate routine consisting of fifty to sixty hours of work in a week that sometimes spilled over into my weekends because the work demanded extra hours to fulfill deadlines. On the other hand my dance studio, Taal, was on and we were getting opportunities to perform at a number of events. I enjoyed the dance more than my work and felt more myself there rather than at my desk. I took a leap, trusting in my natural talents, and decided to quit Deloitte. *Everything began to change... I felt a thirst to know more about myself and to discover my* *inner potential through connecting with my Indian roots and background.*

During the summer, I visited my parents in India. I got my modelling portfolio made. I also met my dance guru, Shri Harish Gangani and started my training in the Jaipur *gharana*, or lineage, of Kathak. When I returned to Los Angeles, I went back to rehearsals with my dance company. Then the call from the talent agency in Delhi came, regarding the movie offer mentioned in the introduction chapter, and it took me into a whirlpool of confusion.

I called my friend Isaah who lived near my apartment in Los Angeles. He told me not to be confused and asked me to meet him. When I pulled up at his house, he was waiting for me on the front porch. I went into his living room and distinctly remember seeing a framed photograph on a corner table of Mata Amritanandamayi, a spiritual leader famously known in South India as the hugging saint mother, 'Amma'. I felt something drawing me to his garden at the back of the house. Before I could understand what my feelings were all about, Isaah handed me a book by the spiritual master, Acharya Rajneesh, or Osho as we know him. I opened it and the first page that I read talked about the energy in the body called *kundalini* and how it can be in seed form or manifested.

I had butterflies in my stomach. I shared the experience I was going through with my friend. He told me to breathe deeply, to allow the feeling to flow through me. He led me to the garden at the back. I took a deep breath… It was a deeply profound moment as I felt a shift. There was something in the air that evening. After my awakening experience, *I felt a deep inner calling to go to India.* I thanked Isaah for the book and left.

The next morning I made a call to my mother and told her that I was moving to India. She was amazed at my quick decision and excited at the same time. Then I called the agency to confirm my acceptance.

I shared the news of the movie offer with my landlady. I was a bit nervous about terminating my lease agreement with her. "What a beautiful girl you are!" she exclaimed. "You are going to India to become an actress!" She hugged me tightly and happily accepted my reason for leaving. She was interesting and bubbly – typical characteristics of Los Angeles. I gave her the mandatory two-week notice to leave the apartment, and she helped me dispose of some of my belongings as I planned my departure.

I sold my car through an internet site and gave some of my furniture and knick-knacks to my friends. All that was left were a few photo albums that I left with my cousin, the elder son of my uncle in Torrance.

Before leaving Los Angeles, I went to Renu's house in South Bay. "You're really going back to India?" She looked at me in disbelief. "Most people dream to be in your shoes – LA, UCLA and Deloitte! But you've envisioned a different journey." I gave her a long, warm hug. It was as if it was all meant to be.

On the way to the airport I recounted all that I was grateful for: being raised in this city of dreams, Los Angeles; my grand teenage life and experiences at UCLA; and working in one of the big five consulting firms before feeling the urge to leave the fast-paced life of America. Am I missing something? Most students in developing countries like India dream to come to the States to graduate from top US universities and work in high-profile corporate America. On the other hand, I had chosen to leave all that behind and to follow a path of discovering myself through my passion for dance and the entertainment world.

It was all so rushed, but I felt a nervous excitement as I sat on the flight. I felt that a new journey was starting for me – perhaps that was why I never looked back. "Good-bye, LA. Your memories will live in me forever." One last thing I thought of while leaving was to thank my parents for taking me back. I was aware that India being a developing country, my decision had its risks, but I promised myself that every time I faced a challenge and thought of returning to the States, I would remind myself of that moment when my heart was filled with the gratitude of going back to my home country.

During the flight I read the entire book *Meditation and the Art of Ecstasy* given by my friend. It was a profound reflection of the living experience within me.

> *"This energy is called kundalini also because the pool of life force, or the seed of life, is precisely located near the sex centre, and it is from here that life expands in all directions."*
>
> **– Osho**

On the way out of the Indira Gandhi International Airport in Delhi, and along the way to my parents' house in Gurugram, I observed the tall trees lining the streets. There were dark clouds covering the setting sun. It was a noticeable change from where I had come. Gurugram, earlier known as Gurgaon, is a city located near the Delhi-Haryana border in northern India.

The staff from the talent agency was already at my parents' house; they were in a rush for me to sign my contract for my role in a Tollywood movie. Jetlagged, I could barely read through the fine print. I slept soundly but woke up the next morning with a headache. There was a thickness from the pollution in the city's air that I was not used to.

My mother and a house maid brought tea to my room. I looked at them strangely. The culture of chai-tea drinking and being served in bed felt different, having lived on my own in Los Angeles for a few years. "I have not been served a cup of tea in ages!" I said to my mother. But I hardly got any time to spend with her. I was ushered out of my parents' house by the agency and into the world of South Indian cinema.

Me in a dupatta sari

My grandparents with my brother and me

School choir

My mom's dresser

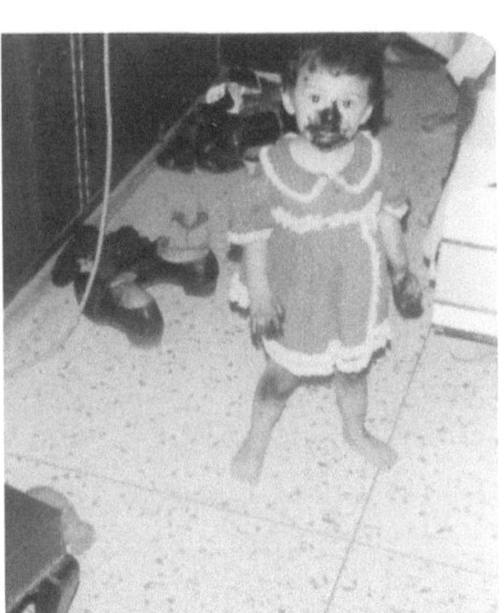

Me messing with shoe polish

Cultural stage performances with my dance group in Los Angeles.

Section 2

Breaking into Movies

"Do what you love and live passionately."

I arrived in Hyderabad in South India and met my co-stars. Hyderabad has one of the major movie industries in India. I was cast opposite Jagapathi Babu who is a veteran actor in Telugu movies. We immediately became friends. Before the shootings, we would get together at the guest house where I was staying in Banjara Hills. The guest house for the artistes was at the same location that was famous for the movie shootings that were held there. Raju Sundaram was our co-star and star choreographer. He would show us the dance moves and we would practice them for the next day's shoot.

Jagapathi Babu and I made a good match on the screen in the movie *Pellaina Kothalo* in which I played the role of a salsa dance instructor. He and the director, Madan, were a great team and my experience of working in the Telugu movie industry started off really well. For one of my songs in the movie, I played the role of Mother Ganga, the personification of the Ganges River in Hindu mythology that flows from the locks of Lord Shiva. It was shot in a studio in Hyderabad.

Before I knew it, the shooting was over. I returned to Delhi. When the movie was released, I received a call from the director as well as my co-stars who congratulated me on a job well done.

My next decision was to star in a multi-star cast movie *Chandrahas*, opposite lead actor Harinath Policherla, who was also the producer. He wanted to make a movie on the great Maratha ruler Chhatrapati Shivaji. I signed a contract for the movie as well as for the shooting at Ramoji Film City and other locations. Ramoji Film City is located in Hyderabad and has been certified by the Guinness World Records as the largest studio complex in the world.

I was flown in from Delhi to the various locations and then flown back during the periodic breaks. Almost half of the movie was shot in Ramoji studios, and then we went to the outdoor locations. We visited hill stations, forts of Shivaji in Maharashtra and various temples. One hit song was shot in a forest.

"Now is my time to give my best on screen," I thought. My looks captured the essence of Indian beauty. As the shooting progressed I became more camera friendly, and by the time the first set of filming was over, my personal makeup team had figured out the look that suited me best.

I played Apsara, one of the lead roles in the movie, alongside my co-stars Harinath Policherla, Superstar Krishna, Abbas, Ravi Prakash and Puneet Issar, all of whom played key roles. The scenes of the movie emerged like the colours of a kaleidoscope. They were filled with the elements of love as well as other emotions and mixed with drama, adventure, comedy and action. I remember with some amusement how, when the director wanted to show me my romantic moves for the songs, he would call the set boys to enact them. At first I would watch carefully to mark my positions, then I would step into the light and the camera would begin to roll.

There was one long dialogue right in the middle of the movie where, after months of searching for the ancient sword, there is a discovery made. It was a dramatic one that lasted around ten minutes and was immediately followed by a song sequence. As the shooting progressed, it got easier for me. The songs were shot towards the end. There are many songs in the movie, but the three that are my favourites are: "O Hamsala..." that was shot in Ramoji Film City; "Idi teeyani teeyani...", a seductive dance sequence choreographed by Tara Master, the legendary dance director; and lastly "Chura chura..." which shows the typical character of a teenage girl in Hyderabad.

Every aspect of the filming – from the dances in the forts, to the stories of the great Maratha ruler, to the songs filled with romance, to the music composed by M.M. Keeravani or M.M. Kreem as he is known – helped me dive into the many facets of Indian culture and heritage. *It felt like living in parallel worlds.*

The movie was released in India on Independence Day that year. It touched the sentiments of the audiences. During the pre-release of the movie, I was given a lot of publicity by the press through newspapers and billboards. The press release of *Chandrahas* went off well. The director, the producer-cum-hero and I were interviewed. Afterwards, the reporters and cameramen crowded around me and requested for some photographs. We stepped out of the conference room and I took a look around the gardens to find a good spot where I could have my pictures taken. My photographs were splashed in important magazines, newspapers and websites.

I was in Hyderabad again on the actual day of the release. The entire city carried beautiful hoardings of the movie. A crowd gathered around me to take my autograph. One girl did not even know the name of the movie, but she was adamant to get my signature. That moment was eye-opening – to see it for myself how stars are passionately revered. "Those were some good days," I sometimes think to myself.

After *Chandrahas*, I took a trip to Mumbai. I met a producer from the movie industry and also spoke with two casting directors. On the phone, one of them posed the question, "Are you willing to compromise?" I realized that the industry was not what I had expected it to be. I took my flight back to Delhi. I accepted another film offer from Hyderabad.

Nearly a decade later, I had the opportunity to go along with filmmaker and artist, Muzaffar Ali, to a festival at the Qutb Shahi Tombs in Hyderabad. The festival was held to commemorate his achievement in Indian cinema, and I was asked to perform to songs from his movie *Umrao Jaan*. Some people in the audience recognized me from my movie days, and I saw my days of being an actor flash in front of my eyes. *It was a moment that seemed like the passing of lives.* I was, at that time, accompanying Muzaffar Ali as an established Kathak dancer.

"It seems in one life multiple stories can exist simultaneously."

An interesting conversation with a dear friend, Meera, happened many years later in Mumbai that I recall here. She and I had connected in Los Angeles when I started my dance company. We talked of our experiences of our acting in Bollywood movies.

"I didn't care much for the gossip on the sets and everyone must've thought I was so into myself," said Meera. I shared one of mine: "Once, at the end of a song, the hero kept holding my hands after the director called cut. I felt so uncomfortable that I ran from the set."

"When I didn't know how to react to situations, I would stay silent," I said, "now my experience in life tells me how I could've handled many of those situations differently. But as long as we give our best in life, that's what matters." I felt very good to have caught up with her, knowing she could relate to what I was saying. "There's no one to impress," she reminded me. "There were of course times when I would really miss my ghungroos and my dancing," I said. Meera understood what I meant, as she too appreciated, and still does, the art of dancing.

She was by then a celebrated, independent belly dancer who also did classical dance and Bollywood shows. She toured regularly. She had finally taken a break, long overdue, to visit India. After going back and forth with our experiences, we acknowledged that our meeting had been well worth it. We were glad we had not missed that chance at a reunion.

"Where are we?" she asked as we looked over the beach in Juhu. We were standing in the courtyard of a hotel. "Oh... it's the Juhu Hotel," I replied. We had arrived there after a long walk on the beach taking pictures. "Wanna eat something?"

I asked. We went to a café across from there and Meera, as usual, got a milkshake full of dates and nuts. I too ordered something healthy. We took our drinks and went down the street.

My mind went back to how we used to dance for hours in her studio upstairs in her loft. She lived a short drive away from my parents' house in Orange County. We had once performed for two thousand people at the Wiltern Theatre in Los Angeles. It was an event held to raise awareness for a cause and was called One Night for India. At the end of our dance, the audience had given us a long applause that even the organizers had been pleasantly surprised.

"Ohmigod! Is that what I think it is?" she asked, pointing to a large billboard. I looked towards the advertisement that read, 'Call this number for a Blind Vodka Date'. It was a Vodka campaign. We laughed, quickly getting into a new mood. "Come!" I grabbed her hand excitedly, "let's pretend we are trying for a Vodka date." "Ok. One sec," she said as she pulled out her phone. "Hello, this is Meera. How can I have a date with you?"

My lesson: **Stand tall in your expression.**

Marriage and Isha

"Our dream is our own, and we are free to take it wherever we want."

After a few releases that put me in the spotlight in the movie industry, I sat at home sifting through the emails sent to me by my business manager. I felt the desire, increasingly, to pursue my art form of Kathak dance. I tied my ghungroos around my ankles. Then I stood up and looked at myself in the mirror. "Yes, Astha, this is what you want to become!" I started dancing. Faster and faster I spun with my hands in the air as the flares of my Anarkali outfit lifted up around me. I stopped turning and looked again into the mirror. Instead of feeling dizzy, I felt exhilarated. I saw a beautiful ballerina-like pose in the mirror, and that was a critical juncture in my life.

In the next year, nearing the occasion of Maha Shivaratri – the auspicious Hindu festival celebrated to honour Lord Shiva – my cousin sister asked me to take a quick trip and join her at the Isha Yoga Center of the Isha Foundation in Coimbatore. She suggested that I attend the 'Great Night of

Shiva' there. I landed in Coimbatore just as the celebrations were commencing. I met many people that night. Amongst them was Nitin.

Sadhguru Jaggi Vasudev, the founder of the Isha Foundation, is a practitioner of yoga and meditation. He is also a spiritual leader. Every year the festivities, held outside the Dhyanalinga Temple for Lord Shiva worshipers, begin at 6 pm. The whole night is filled with melodies by music bands from all over the country including one from the centre itself called, Sounds of Isha, consisting mostly of monks. The celebrations continue till the next morning, and most of the crowds stay up in the night dancing to the music of the bands on stage and visiting the food stalls.

Nitin was tall and had beautiful, dark eyes. He also had a big heart. I met him on that special occasion of Maha Shivaratri. He was a volunteer with the foundation and followed the Isha discipline strictly. When he and I talked, we suddenly had an unusual chemistry between us. It also turned out that we had many things to talk about. Our conversation was curtailed by my cousin who pulled me away to show me the newly-built ayurveda spa. Nitin and I decided we would talk again in the days to come. Then he visited Delhi. He came over to my parents' house and we had a chance to talk more in detail. It led to a curiosity that turned, three months later, into a marriage proposal.

I remember Sadhguru's words as we touched his feet to get his blessings, "If you really enjoy being with each other," he looked at Nitin, "the two of you should get married and live at the centre." But our plan was to live in Delhi.

A few months later, Nitin's parents came over to Gurugram and a date was fixed. We had a grand wedding at the Centaur Hotel, Delhi, and it was attended by family, friends and other guests from both sides.

I was excited about being an Indian bride and had hired the best makeup artist, Ambika Pillai.

In the evening, before my wedding party, Ambika looked at me. "Try to stay still." She had to remind me repeatedly as she did my eyes. I could not contain my excitement. As she applied mascara, I tried not to take a peek at myself in the mirror. But I could not contain myself any longer. I asked if I could take one quick look. I blushed, looking at myself as a bride. I told her to continue. She completed my entire wedding makeup in one hour. A few minutes later, my driver was at the door and I was all set to go to the wedding venue.

In the car, my paternal grandmother sat in the back seat. She looked at me and said, "Did you think I was not going to come to your wedding?" I laughed. I was so happy that my mother had arranged for her pick-up and that she was accompanying me. Then she looked at my wedding outfit and said, "Yellow?" "Dadi, it's the colour I chose," I said, remembering having seen my mother's pink and red lehenga when I was a kid. I had designed my own lehenga. "*Chalo, tumhara zamana to wohi karta hai jo tum chahte ho*," she said, meaning that my generation does what we want.

At Centaur, guests had begun arriving on the lawn where the event was planned. I could see members of my family standing at a distance, glittering in their saris. A cousin sister-in-law saw me getting out of the car and started running towards me. I dashed through a side entrance of the hotel as I heard her calling out my name. “I’ll just come!” I yelled and hurried to my suite. Moments later, my mother walked in. She looked at me adoringly, and then she handed me my jewellery and a pair of gold-coloured heels that matched my attire perfectly.

For Nitin and me, our discipline, or *sadhana*, became a daily part and parcel of our married life. The term *sadhana* refers to the discipline of yoga that we followed along with our lifestyle. Even our individual professions came under that. My habits slowly changed and I began to have a holistic approach to life. My morning routine included my yoga practice along with my *riyaz*, or dance practice. My dance teacher would visit in the mornings for my *riyaz*. I refer to my dance guru in the system of the *guru-shishya parampara* – the teacher-disciple tradition. Once I started my daily practice with a disciplined approach, the entire charm of partying at night naturally fell away.

Shri Harish Gangani of the Jaipur *gharana* or lineage, was my first dance teacher in India. I was content to be under him. I would dance for hours under his able guidance, with my ghungroos firmly tied to my ankles, to hone and perfect my skills. I was very keen to learn the intricacies of the art from him.

Seeing my interest, Harish Gangani, whom I respectfully addressed as Guru*ji,* encouraged me to perform on stage as a solo artiste. Right from the beginning he gave me education and training to build my repertoire or *talim*. A year later I performed at the Epicentre, a new cultural establishment in Gurugram which housed an exhibition centre and an auditorium. Soon after, he presented me at the Habitat Centre in New Delhi.

Once I got used to performing on stage, it felt like it could go on forever.

The first time that I performed with Guruji, he had me enter the stage holding my *ghunghat*, the veil of my lehenga, in my hands as I came into the light. The piece was about Lord Krishna stopping a young damsel midway as she fills her pail with water. I played the part of the damsel. In the next show where Guruji was performing, someone in the audience requested to have me perform one particular piece on stage. People especially loved seeing my expressions in a *thumri*, which is a devotional or romantic song sung in a particular style. Guruji's wife came running to me backstage and said, "Quickly, get ready!" I was taken aback. "Now?" I asked. I was not prepared. "You can't refuse when people in the audience make a special request," she said. I changed my attire and did the thumri that he had taught me so lovingly. For my next show, I prepared my own *bandishi* thumri with Guruji's help. *Bandishi* is about evoking feelings in a repetitive manner.

After a few more years of training with him, I decided to hold my own stage production. I raised some funds through an organization in Gurugram and presented my new concept on Buddhism at the India International Centre in New Delhi. My guru shone through me as I held my first production in a Buddhist style called Sancarana, or silent movement, on the Japanese Haiku form of poetry. Soon Guruji sent me to work exclusively for the Ministry of Culture under Sangeet Natak Akademi in their Repertory Company comprising, mostly, solo Kathak dancers from different cities. That was a big step in my career as a solo artiste.

Nitin was supportive of my dance and would usually be busy on his own assignments at work. My parents-in-law too said to me, “Don’t miss even one day of your dance practice.”

Meanwhile, I started going more regularly to meet another lady who became my guru after I joined the Repertory under the Ministry of Culture. She was a great dancer of the Lucknow tradition of Kathak. I will talk about her in detail later. Most days when Nitin would leave for work, I would go to my guru’s place to learn. Sometimes I would spend the weekend with her. One day I approached her and asked her to help me conceptualize my ideas on a production that involved Sufi mystics. From then on she helped me in my discipline through the years that I grew as a young dancer.

Once, while we sat in her flat in Malviya Nagar, she shared her perspective, “We are so lucky to have our dance.” She told me about the time when she first met her husband. He was an actor and they worked in the same building. They liked each other instantly but were hesitant to get married. One day, as she sat down to eat, she realized that she could not be eating alone for the rest of her life. Finally, the two of them agreed to get married. I hugged her. Her simplicity touched my heart. I respected her and admired her style of dance that I slowly picked up as I spent more time with her.

When she had other engagements and could not meet me, I would set up a photograph of my idol, the classical dance maestro, Pt. Birju Maharaj with his first female disciple, Sashwati Sen in front of my mirror and dance as I had seen them do on stage. I loved the way he presented *nakhra*, or playful seduction, in his dance. I found his feet and hand movements near effortless. I remember once someone describing his dance movements as the tinkling of bells or even the sound of waves on a shore. I had attended some of his workshops in Delhi and taken particular notice of how he taught his senior students.

One day Lila, a friend of mine in Gurugram, invited me to her house. She had recently delivered a baby boy whom she had named after a Japanese warrior. He was the cutest thing I had ever seen. She began to leave me with him when needing to go out for any work. He would fall asleep in his stroller, his eyes fluttering a little just before drifting. I would watch carefully till he dozed off and then go into the living room and practice my dance routine. Entering through the glass doors in the living room, I would stand in front of a ceramic statue of a dancing couple and take my stance. I practiced for all my shows of that season right there in Lila's living room.

More about Isha

In keeping with the yoga tradition at Isha, Nitin wanted to return to the centre every few months. In addition, there was an annual event held every March. "Aum Namah Shivaya!" came the chanting of a group of monks sitting behind the base drummer. Suddenly, a haunting flute melody came from the back with the loud thumping of beats on a large base drum. The ambience was serene and divine.

At the centre, Nitin was focused on his meditation and spiritual practice while I spent most of my time doing riyaz in my room. He would take long walks around the Dhyanalinga temple. The Dhyanalinga temple has the largest sculpture of the Lingam – a representation of the Hindu god Shiva – that I have ever seen in any temple in India. We would walk around it and place our lit copper vessels at the base of the sculpture that was surrounded by lotus flowers floating in a body of water. People would prostrate themselves in front of the temple or in front of the statue of Patanjali at the gates on the way out. As we walked past the tamarind tree outside the temple complex the first time, Nitin had stopped me midway to say, “That’s Patanjali. He was the one to bring yoga into the world.”

We would also take long walks around the complex. There were times when one of the monks would stop us along the way, “Hey Nitin! What are you doing?” They would chat while I looked around. The symbol of the snake in the décor throughout the Isha premises is representative of the Shiva tradition. The figures look unimaginably real in places. We would walk into the dining hall and usually sit across from each other on mats placed on the ground. Volunteers would come around and serve us food. Once my parents-in-law called me and asked, “How are you two doing?” “Fine,” I said. “He is busy with his things. I am busy with mine.” “That’s good,” they said. “As long as you two are happy together.”

However, from the beginning, Nitin and I started going our separate ways. He got a new job in marketing with a company and I was focused on my dancing and on developing my skills as a performer. On hindsight, Nitin and I were better off as friends. Perhaps that was what it was supposed to be, but we had rushed into something else. He was a sort of introvert, led by his discipline for sadhana. He spent more of his energy and time enjoying his own work, and the two of us just dived more and more into our separate passions and had lesser things to talk to each other about. When I started realizing that we were more into our own worlds rather than our families or future together, I began worrying and understood it was not a relationship I wanted to be in.

A few years into our marriage, just before Nitin and I parted, I wrote a letter to Sadhguru asking for advice regarding my life going forward. He replied: “Focus on your dance.”

I remember the night before my wedding: I danced to a song composed by Pt. Birju Maharaj from the Hindi movie, *Devdas*. Of course I danced at my own pre-wedding celebrations! I had prepared numerous dance sequences that wove on and off the dance floor. My cousins and I even copied the facial expressions of the actors in the movies. By the end of the occasion the men of the family were all on the dance floor as well. The whole experience was memorable for the guests who attended. For our wedding party, at my special request, we had called a celebrated singer, Papon and his group, The East India Company, from Assam. I had also asked the decorators to use peacock feathers all over in the decor.

That was a walk down our wedding festivities before I take the reader through the next part.

Nitin and I took one last trip together in the summer before our separation. We decided to fly to Lebanon for a friend’s wedding, but before heading there, we went to Jordan to see Petra. We wound through the narrow rock walls at the entrance of Petra and arrived at the city centre. All around us there were tourists taking photographs with the rock carvings. Much to our surprise the entire city, built by the Nabateans, is carved out of stone.

A Bedouin with a donkey approached us and gave us a tour of the ruins. We spent time with the Bedouins of that area who became very friendly with us. On our return to Delhi after that trip, *I had a new desire to travel and get to know my real self.*

Did I have the courage and strength to admit to myself that I needed to separate and make progress on my own? And that, perhaps, my marriage was a hindrance? The blessings that I received from Nitin and his family in the form of their encouragement in my dance journey, were enough for me to fulfill my life's purpose at that time. A thousand opinions of friends and family come one's way; the decision is never easy. And although, at the time, it appears to be the best and only solution, one has to question oneself honestly: "Am I throwing a good marriage away?"

I decided to move away, and soon after we parted, I began to rise professionally from the years of training I had given to my dance.

The trauma remains… and probably always will as a marriage is never meant to end. If someone asked me how I felt when I attended events and weddings and saw other people, especially women, enjoying the so-called bliss of married life, and also saw children playing under the watchful and proud eyes of their parents, I would say I was complacent for a while. However, after some time, the effects of my broken marriage started troubling me.

I believe one should think it through thoroughly before deciding on a divorce and choosing to live life alone thereafter, as it is mostly not easy. If it is one's decision, so be it, but be aware that in many cases there is a price to pay with regard to what society thinks. Also, it may take time to realize the after-effects of this life-changing process, and one may not grasp the outcome of the decision until much later. In the Indian culture, even in today's world, in some societies there is a stigma attached to divorce. In my belief it should be the last resort to a disturbed relationship.

For years I hid behind my dance – an ancient classical art form carried on by people who usually gain tremendous respect in society. The world accepted the image it saw of me, in my performances, as a contribution to my culture. In the coming chapters, I have covered some of my accomplishments as an artiste and have attempted to give glimpses of some of my tours.

How can one eventually repair one's life and dream again after such a life-changing event? To those in a similar situation as I was in, I say: find your strength in either an art form or some form of devotion. Any kind of creative art form is not an escape from the hurt but rather a way to deal with emotions.

Spirituality is a path that few choose to follow, but it can give tremendous inner strength and willpower. It helps in this journey that requires great patience to overcome the challenges. With faith and patience, I waited for my time again.

I have always firmly believed in the institution of marriage, there is no doubt about that. But it must be with the **right person**, one with similar values and goals. A strong base is fundamental to a relationship. And like a tree, a marriage must be able to bend with the storms that are sure to come.

"There is a space within us beyond all attachments."

Sannyas Initiation

"Life is an open secret...

All that you need are the correct eyes to see the truth."

– Osho

This chapter is about my Sannyas initiation at the Osho ashram. I was at home in Gurugram, fast asleep. A white beam of light shone from above. I was talking to someone. He leaned over and said something to me. We looked ahead. There was someone with a long beard at a distance looking at us.

I suddenly woke up. It was 9 am. I put my ghungroos on and started my riyaz. Two hours passed. I washed my face and went into the kitchen. I was making my porridge when I looked at my phone. There were seven missed calls.

As I started returning the calls, I saw a message from Swami Ravindra from the Osho Centre, called ashram, in New Delhi. "Have you arrived in Delhi yet?" it read. I called him. "How was your trip?" he asked. "It was fantastic," I lied. He continued, "What are you doing now?" "Nothing, just making breakfast," I replied. "Come over to the ashram," he said. "It's ok. I'm tired." I hung up the phone immediately.

A few months earlier, during the summer, my mother's side of the family had taken a vacation at Chail, a hill station near Shimla. It was my cousin sister's wedding anniversary and she had flown in from London for the celebrations. We were around forty of us on that trip. I packed my ghungroos too as I thought there would be nothing like doing riyaz up in the mountains. We drove up to a beautiful resort in Chail, large enough to accommodate the whole family, and checked into our individual cottages.

On the first morning, my cousin sister announced that a healing 'laughter meditation' session had been arranged for us in the hall downstairs. It was to be conducted by Swami Ravindra. As we stepped inside the hall, some of us were still rubbing our eyes. The session started but it did not seem like meditation to many, and after some time, only a few of us remained in the hall till the end of it.

On the night of the anniversary party, everyone enjoyed themselves on the dance floor. During dinner, I was seated at the same table as Swami Ravindra. He began laughing loudly over the music as he said something to my mother who sat next to him. I could not hear him. Then he looked at me and said, "Now I know why I came to this family reunion!" He started laughing again.

Back in my kitchen, as I stirred my porridge that morning, I remembered all that had happened on the Chail trip. By the evening I changed my mind and decided to call Swami Ravindra. "How do I arrive at the ashram?" I wrote down what he said on a piece of paper. "You go past the village and turn left. Then you drive past the bus stand. There, on your left, you will see a big gate that reads Osho Centre. Tell the guards you are there for the meditation. If you get lost, call me."

I called my driver to pick me up the next morning. He knew the whereabouts of the ashram. "Ma'am, I have heard of it," he said as he wound the car through the lanes of Jhatikra Village in the subdistrict of Najafgarh. The centre was located near the outskirts of West Delhi. It had fields all around filled with mustard plants. I arrived in broad daylight to the sound of wind chimes over the dining hall. Swami Ravindra sat on a chair in the company of a few people. I approached him and gave him a hug. It is how all the Osho people meet. The chimes kept tinkling overhead and a large portrait of Osho stood out in the dining area. Spiritual teacher Osho, also known as Acharya Rajneesh, lived in the years 1931 to 1990, and the West Delhi ashram is one of the many that have been built to propagate his teachings.

Everyone was laughing; I did not know why. Swami Ravindra left the others to show me my room. A lady walked in quietly behind us and placed her stick beside one of the beds. Swami Ravindra turned around to introduce us. "This is Ma Astha. She has come from Delhi. She is a great dancer. The two of you will be sharing this room." The lady looked at me and asked me my name again. I pronounced it slowly and clearly for her. Swami Ravindra told me she had come from Europe, and being deep into her meditation practice, she was not to be disturbed. I went to my side of the room. Looking back at her, I saw that she had a deep and amicable smile. It left a mark on me.

I followed the routine of the Osho meditation techniques to the best of my ability. On the second day of my arrival at the ashram, I attended therapy sessions that included dancing and speaking in gibberish, a nonsensical language. Osho's meditations focus on catharsis and the silencing of the mind through such methods.

I met a gentleman who was tall and had sharp facial features. During lunch, he sat at the same table with a group of us and listened intently to our talk. When I got up to leave, he stood up too. He stopped me at the door and asked my name. With his hand on his heart he said, "I am Basant. So what brings you to this side of town?" "Nothing," I replied. "Ok," he nodded. He gave me his number. He was a lawyer by profession. "If you need any help you can call me."

On the next weekend, I decided to go to the ashram again. There was another gentleman facilitating the meditation course for that weekend. I smiled at him on my way to my room. I wore my customary robe and walked into the large meditation hall called Buddha Hall. Once the session began, I immersed myself in the music and let myself free in my dance. I enjoyed the feel of the environment.

Afterwards, lawyer Basant appeared before me. We stood there facing each other. Without saying anything he introduced me to someone else who gave me a warm hug. The next morning he arrived in the meditation hall for the session at the same time that I did. The music started, and I closed my eyes and began to dance. When I opened my eyes, I saw everyone dancing around me. Round and round we went. The whole Buddha Hall was, in a way, spinning around us. In the evening we met again in the meditation hall. We sat with our eyes closed. The bell rang. "My dear Sannyasins…" It was Osho's voice from a large projector. To Osho, the word 'sannyas' meant 'seeking the truth'. And, most importantly, he was all for "whatever your truth might be."

Sannyas Celebration

The next day was a Sunday. There were a lot more people at the ashram for the Sannyas celebration as well as the evening Buddha meditation. They checked into their rooms and came out dressed in maroon robes. In the evening, they changed into another colour. My name was signed in the register for the Sannyas initiation. As we danced in the Buddha Hall, the lights dimmed. There were three cushions in front of me. I sat on one and looked up at Osho's framed picture. *As I looked at his face, my heart surrendered, and tears flowed down.*

I knew I would be getting my garland as a symbol of my initiation into the Osho Neo-Sannyas group. Soon they called me to the front of the hall and gave me initiation, explaining to me the requirements of the routine that I was to follow. When I came away, I saw everyone dancing in a group. They made a circle around me. Lawyer Basant and an older lady called Ma Jyoti welcomed me into the group. They held my hand and all of us danced together.

After the celebration, a sweet older gentleman stopped me on my way to my room. He asked, "It seems we have met somewhere before this. Have you been to the Pune ashram?" I shook my head to say no. I was rushing to change for dinner, so I thanked him and left. Later that evening, I was asked to go to the facilitator's room to collect my certificate. I looked at the document. They had engraved my name with the words, 'Dance your way to God'.

My initiation was a step deeper into my own inner journey and a chance to re-unite with my master. The next day, at lunch, when someone asked me what I liked about the place, my reply was immediate and with no hesitation, "I feel at home for once in my life."

Osho's messages rang deep and clear when we heard his voice, and I had no doubt that his thought process rang a bell in my own mind. I was visiting the ashram with no expectation and was trying his meditations with a non-partial attitude. There were methods of awareness and 'no-mind' that were actually bringing a stillness to my own mind. So, putting aside all controversies with regard to Osho's teachings, I was following my own purpose.

I connected deeply with a few of his practices that came naturally to me. There were some practices only about dance called Nataraj Meditation. I could finally feel the wind beneath my wings, and I touched those heights of ecstasy that I had felt when I was leaving Los Angeles. I realized I was led to Osho, and that realization led me to meet many other people who became my new family.

In those days, my paternal grandmother lived in a large portion of our old house in Greater Kailash in New Delhi. She lived alone ever since my grandfather passed away almost ten years before then. One day, I went to visit her and she told me that she was getting tired of living all by herself and managing such a big house. I jumped at the chance and asked if I could remodel a section of it for my dance studio. It was a great idea I thought. She gave me her permission.

Dadi moved to Gurugram temporarily as the renovation of the Greater Kailash house began. It took nearly two years to complete. It was during that time that Nitin and I went through a very cordial divorce process – an amicable separation that led to a new turn in my life. I was no longer in a compromising place in my heart. After meeting the Bedouins in Jordan that summer, something within me was ready to move on. I had sat on that airplane on my return to Delhi and had told myself that I was ready to embrace my circumstances and whatever came my way. Nitin and I went our separate directions with no hard feelings.

Dadi's house was transformed. We began with the uplifting of the old living room, changed the ceilings and repainted the interiors. I set up full-length, wall-to-wall mirrors in the living room for my dance. I called it my studio. I also made a drastic change to the kitchens which I converted into fully-equipped modular ones with new tiles and counters. The rooms that lay around a central courtyard were improved as well.

Meanwhile, during that transition period, I stayed at my parents' house and visited my dance guru in Malviya Nagar during the week. Since I had started learning from her, I was picking up speed and grace. In addition, I visited the Osho ashram quite often, mostly on the weekends. Osho's evening *satsang*, or spiritual meetings, were about discourse and dance. *His primary focus on dance and celebration seemed to go hand in hand with my dance as my way of life.* There seemed a nice synchronicity between my riyaz and my meditation practice.

After the renovation, my dadi and I moved back into the Greater Kailash house. But, somehow, things did not seem to sit well with my family. There began a new conflict at home. First and foremost, why had I picked Osho? And, secondly, why was I not focused on seeking a new man now that a year had passed since my divorce with Nitin?

For a moment I would like to answer the question: Why Osho? I have realized that the controversies surrounding Osho stand known to everyone. His teachings, however, remain useful for seekers like me. I have listened to Osho. His discourses, as I have experienced, bring clarity to the mind. I looked forward to visiting the centre particularly to listen to the discourses. Certain talks that are etched in my mind are about Meera Bai, Kabir, Guru Nanak, and many other saints.

There was another centre near my house in Gurugram that was affiliated with Osho called Zorba the Buddha. Many of us from the two centres – West Delhi and Gurugram, travelled to Goa, Pune and various other Osho ashrams where a similar method of Osho's meditations is followed. In Pune, we landed at the airport at 7 pm and visited the ashram the next day. Without going into the details of the visit I would like to mention how, when I sat in the meditation hall and closed my eyes, I felt aligned with my master.

Things at home remained as they were. My parents' pressure on me to remarry continued at a subconscious level, *but I felt free as I was aligned with my purpose.*

Passage to Braj

"Love is like the depths of an ocean that no one dares to cross."

'Braj' is another name for the holy town of Vrindavan, also spelt Brindavan, that refers to the earth of this town that the people here worship.

Vrindavan can take one deeper into devotion of an art form. For someone like me who has taken classical dance seriously, it brings out the true devotion in my dance form.

On the path of *nritya*, or classical dance, this holy town is often mentioned in the songs that are sung. It is said that the dancing god, Lord Krishna, came to the earth to dance and love His *gopis*, the maidens of Vrindavan. The town seems to have a significant mythological impact on both religion and dance as it is the place Lord Krishna came to soon after his birth.

My personal journey continued, and I went to Vrindavan in the Mathura District of Uttar Pradesh. The following story will give a background on the experiences that led me there.

My performance was held at the tomb of Raskhan, the celebrated poet of India during the Mughal reign of

King Akbar. The poet himself had been a devotee of Lord Krishna. He died in Vrindavan in 1628 and his tomb is located twenty kilometres outside of Mathura.

The singer and musical artiste for the performance, J.S.R. Madhukar, is from Mumbai, but he has his roots in Vrindavan. He belongs to a family of Braj *rasikas*, or the *rasikas* of Vrindavan as they are called. Rasikas are devotees who seek worship and connect with the Lord through forms of art. His father, up until his passing, had been a saint of Vrindavan and a true devotee of Lord Krishna. Madhukar continues to keep the family tradition alive by doing yearly concerts at many locations in Vrindavan.

As I bent down to tie my ghungroos, I saw an elderly man with a long white beard sitting next to Madhukar. Both of us looked at each other and nodded a greeting. He was Swami Hit Kinkar Sevak Charan Maharaj, the leader of a spiritual tradition and a revered person in Vrindavan. I stood up to dance.

Atop the tomb structure, I began taking Kathak spins. On and on I went as the music flowed from the group of musicians sitting at the base of the structure. I continued with my expressions and dance to the lyrics of Madhukar's songs. Below me, in the audience, were crowds from Mathura and the nearby towns, saints and devotees alike. As I finished my spins, the eyes of the audience were on me. After the concert, just outside the tomb, a feast was laid out for all the devotees.

On the way back to Vrindavan, we were four of us in Madhukar's car. Madhukar sat behind the wheel and I was beside him in the passenger seat. Swami Sevak Charan sat directly behind me and a disciple next to him. "Where are we going?" asked Swamiji in a very soft, barely audible voice. "We are going to drop you first then we will take the artiste back to her hotel," Madhukar replied. We stopped the car outside Swamiji's residence. He stepped out slowly as his attendants came forward to help him.

"Who is he?" I asked as Madhukar drove off towards my hotel. "He was a dear friend of Pitaji, my father," he paused, "I have many more saints you can meet," he said as we arrived at our destination. In the evening I spent my time relaxing in my room.

The next morning, on my request, Madhukar called Swamiji on the phone and asked his permission for me to meet him at his residence. I went over and told Swamiji about my parents and their pressure on me to get married. I shared with him that I wanted my freedom to lead my own life, but how, sometimes, the conservative approach of my parents was difficult for me to manage. Addressing me as a daughter, he said, "Beti, what is it that is stopping you from achieving your freedom?" I stayed silent. "You need more spiritual practice to understand." Just then, Madhukar arrived. Swamiji began chatting with him about the nitty-gritty of the ashram affairs. They talked endlessly about the families of devotees in Vrindavan. I started to get impatient.

"Let's go," Madhukar finally said as he stood up and, in keeping with the Hindu tradition of showing respect to an elder, he bent down and touched Swamiji's feet. The simple man was dressed in modest white clothes: a light shirt and a one-piece garment wrapped around his waist. Swamiji's eyes looked piercingly at me. As I got into the car, I looked back.

On our way to the hotel, Madhukar talked about the great families of rasikas who lived in Vrindavan and how I should meet them. Not wishing to go into too much of that, I tried to ignore his suggestion.

In the next some months after that concert, Madhukar and I kept going back for similar performances in key places in the land of Braj.

I was in Gurugram at my parents' house when I received a phone call to attend a five-day retreat at the Hit Sadhana Mandal – the forest ashram and personal residence of Swami Sevak Charan Maharaj on the outskirts of Vrindavan near ISKCON Temple.

I knew it was not going to be easy to convince my parents about my attending the retreat; they had earlier expressed their concern regarding what I was trying to achieve by visiting such places. The next day, when I got the opportunity, I asked them. They gave me a questioning look. I quickly packed my bags and went out of the door. The drive took me just a couple of hours to get to Swamiji's residence.

The forest area surrounding the residence was densely covered with trees. Monkeys sat menacingly on branches. They jumped from tree to tree and peeked down, ready to pounce at their first opportunity. As I walked quickly through the forest, two of the creatures swooped down to grab my bag. I clutched my belongings and ran, just managing to reach the entrance of the main building unharmed. It was a narrow escape.

I was one of six people who attended the retreat. I entered into a hall where Swamiji sat on a thick mattress on the floor. The rest of us sat in front of him as he addressed us. When food was served, we silently ate what was put on our plates and then took our dishes outside for cleaning. The monkeys were all around the place. They were a nuisance so we had to be very observant of where we were walking. As I finished washing my plate, I avoided one staring at me and quickly went inside.

I looked up at a photograph on the wall next to the kitchen. There was a beautiful lady in the frame. "She must have been his wife," I thought.

I went to Swamiji and naturally bent down to obtain his blessings. He was thin and walked with a stick. He was dressed in pure white clothes, the same as when I met him the first time. "Yes beti," he said warmly as he looked at me. "Swamiji, where do you want me to sleep?" I looked around, taking in all that was there in the hall.

I was guided to a room next to the hall. It was vacant and I laid my duffel bag on a mattress. I looked around, not sure how I would be able to sleep without air conditioning or a room cooler. I was completely uncertain of what lay ahead for me.

Adjacent to the hallway was the kitchen. Mamaji, the elder brother of Swamiji's late wife, took care of the affairs of the kitchen and the main gate. He was the caretaker of the property. In fact he slept near the main gate. Every morning he would enter the hallway through a side entrance with a bag in his hand and head straight to the kitchen. He would clean the kitchen and then cook for Swamiji his favourite meal of *chappatis*, an Indian whole-grain bread, with lentils and vegetables. He would soften the *chappatis* by soaking them in water. Watching him every day, I became familiar with the routine. I began looking after Swamiji's needs, at times, when

Mamaji was busy. Swamiji mostly stayed in the hall and even slept there, except for the times when he was taking rounds of the entire area comprising the temple, the meditation hall and the forest.

During the retreat, I slept on the mattress in my room. In my view, I was willing to adjust according to the circumstances at the ashram so long as I could obtain Swamiji's teachings. He took care of me like a father would. He started teaching me about the tradition of Vrindavan's process of self-transformation.

I visited Swamiji at his ashram quite often after the retreat days. At home, I started feeling disconnected with my parents who clearly did not understand the path I was taking in spirituality. They were concerned about my safety and future.

I remember what the great poet Raskhan wrote as part of a monologue on the nature of divine love:

"Love is inaccessible, incomparable, immeasurable

It is like the ocean -

He who comes to its shore will not go back..."

Whenever I read those lines, only one thing comes to mind: **As a traveler on the mystical path begins to understand the nature of true love, to him or her all things external begin to lose their meaning.**

Life as a Disciple

"If you are sincerely looking for your higher purpose, ask as a disciple."

After my performance in Vrindavan, I naturally had songs of J.S.R. Madhukar running through my mind and in my ears as I had his entire album playing on my laptop throughout the day. The devotion that came through in the lyrics, especially in two of his songs: "Joi joi pyaro kare, soi moi bhave" and "Ras ke bhare tere dou nain," really touched me. I realized that I had never understood Lord Krishna until I understood His relationship with His beloved consort Radha. *The seeker in me longed for more of the knowledge of divine love.* And that is what led me to Vrindavan in the coming months.

My longest stay in Vrindavan was for one month at a stretch. It was right in the peak of summer in the month of June. That was the time I came under the guidance of Swami Sevak Charan Maharaj whom I began calling Babaji, or simply Baba. On that visit in June, I waited for someone to escort me to the main building of the ashram. The monkeys in the forest were growing very fast in number.

At Babaji's ashram, I got into the habit of waking up at 4:30 am. Babaji would sit with a small group of us on the terrace outside the temple and demonstrate the correct way of doing *pranayama*, or breathing exercises, leading into prayers that started off our day. Usually he would then take us around the temple, pointing out various spots that were conducive for meditation. He started me on bead-counting on the sacred string of prayer beads or *mala* – counting first from one to one hundred and eight, and then counting in reverse. That completed one round of counting. There were a hundred and eight such rounds to be done. It brought a sense of balance within me and built in me an appetite to know more about the Vrindavan tradition.

I would assist Mamaji in the kitchen, serving Baba his meals whenever possible. The temperatures were extremely high, and there was nothing much to keep us cool except for the diet which included lots of fruits from the trees in the forest. Meanwhile, I also got used to sleeping on a mattress, sometimes moving it around to get as much air as possible from the fan. Those peak summer months were relentless with temperatures crossing forty degrees Celsius on some days. I, somewhat, got used to the monkeys and learnt to carry a stick every time I stepped outside.

Babaji explained to me the intrinsic union of beloved Lord Krishna and His gopis. He drew their figures within a circle in a symbolic fashion to help me understand. He mentioned that the circle of life keeps repeating itself in an unending manner. It reminded me of the same thing that I had learnt as a child and also a similar concept of Hinduism that I had been exposed to at UCLA.

Most days, when Baba would instruct us, we would be sitting either on the terrace outside the temple where the breeze came through or in the meditation hall. I would hand him his stick so he could get up, and we would then walk back towards the main building from the temple.

One of his other disciples, Dheeraj, asked Baba if he could visit some of the temples nearby and pay his respects to the priests. I suddenly stood up. "Do you want to go with him?" Baba asked me. "As you say, Babaji," I replied.

We completed our work in the kitchen and went out for the first time into the lanes of Vrindavan. It happened to be on the occasion of Radha Ashtami – the birthday celebration of Lord Krishna's consort, Radha. The streets were crowded with people from the adjoining cities who were visiting. Everyone was screaming and shouting to get past the crowds and into the temples. We got off our rickshaw a few blocks away and went on foot to the Radhavallabh temple.

We entered from the rear side. There was a lot of pushing and shoving as people walked towards the inner sanctum, singing prayers loudly and in unison. We broke away from the crowds when a priest, who had been informed by Babaji's ashram, came to greet us and take us into the sanctum sanctorum that was cordoned off by a rope. I had a few moments in front of the deity. I closed my eyes... Then the priest held the rope for us to exit. Next we were led up to the room right above the inner sanctum. I hesitated as I entered and stood in front of the head priest of the temple who was also the main authority of the Radhavallabh tradition.

We paid our respects, and as we were leaving, the head priest pointed towards his library. "It is important for a disciple to get the correct information from the scriptures right from the beginning." "Yes Acharya," said Dheeraj. We quickly left. I followed Dheeraj, and once we were out of the temple, we had a sigh of relief.

It was then that I understood why Baba kept us from stepping out of his ashram. He did not want us to get lost in the many traditions that prevailed in the holy town.

We got back to the ashram late at night. I remember waking up the next morning feeling fresh and alive. I went out into the garden towards the meditation hall. For the first time *I felt as if time had stopped and all that remained in that moment was me.* I felt a sense of vigour and joy. The experience of the previous day had refreshed me. However, Madhukar's words came back to me. I remembered his warning. "There is always another saint up the street for those on the spiritual path. If you want, I can take you," he had said with a wink. "No thanks, I don't wish to be confused," I had said, looking away.

A message for seekers on the spiritual path: People will try to get you interested in their systems or beliefs as it is in their interest to make you their disciple. **Be wary of traditions that are not your path. Stay focused on your own journey.**

I remembered a quote by Rumi: "Dance, when you are broken open. Dance, if you have torn the bandage off. Dance in the middle of the fighting. Dance in your blood. Dance when you are perfectly free."

My search had led me to Vrindavan and I had joined a caravan of seekers. I was carefree and moving through life with a powerful new energy. I had never imagined it as even a possibility as I had only heard of Lord Krishna in poems till then, and there I was, having just dived into the Vrindavan spiritual tradition under the blessings of Swami Sevak Charan. *Being in the moment is when you are truly in divine love.*

The philosophy that I picked up in Vrindavan, in relation to divinity, seemed to fit into the fabric of life that I had already understood. But many questions remained. "How does one integrate this into one's daily life?" Such questions remained unanswered for a long time. "The answers don't come easily," Babaji said, "seekers have to continue to find their answers."

While my time in Vrindavan was mostly positive and helped me in my journey, I encountered an unpleasant experience after which I decided that it was time for me to move on from there. One day, a new disciple arrived at the ashram. He carried gifts that he laid at Babaji's feet. Babaji immediately welcomed him and told him to sit down. I watched the clock above them tick as the two conversed with each other. It got past dinnertime; I began getting concerned. Finally the disciple left, and Babaji and I sat down to eat. As usual, after serving us, Mamaji took his dinner outside and sat near the main gate. Without saying much, Babaji gave me his blessings before I went to my room.

The next day the disciple visited again. After a few more days, he came with his wife. Her wrists tinkled with lots of bangles as she walked in. From the kitchen I could see her bending down to touch Babaji's feet. I walked past them without saying anything and went outside to where the dishes were stacked for washing. The water was flowing. As usual the tap had been meddled with by monkeys. I quickly closed it. I went back inside to find that the couple had left. Afterwards, I asked Baba about them. He said they were devotees and that they would bring good luck to his centre.

The following day, the couple came again. I noticed that the man carried some documents with him and I overheard some parts of their conversation with Baba. I also noted the sari that the wife wore – it was patterned in bright jewelled colours. Babaji seemed happy when they thanked him and left.

In the next month, there was a feast arranged for the devotees of the ashram as well as for those of the neighboring centres that were affiliated with Babaji's tradition. It was a yearly occurrence. I had just arrived from Delhi after much resistance from my parents. All of us sat down to eat while the helpers served food on our plates. Halfway into my meal, I felt sick and ran to the bathroom. I had to hold myself steady against a wall. There was something seriously wrong.

I prayed to god to help me.

A few other devotees had a similar reaction. We were rushed to the nearest hospital in Mathura and given emergency care and put on intravenous drip. At that moment my phone rang showing my father's number. I explained to him what had happened. We had to stay in the intensive care unit all night as we had had a severe case of food poisoning. The next day, my father picked me up and took me home.

Going back to what had happened the previous day, there was talk around the ashram that the couple had poisoned our food. They probably had their eyes on the beautiful property that was Babaji's and had tried to cause disruption.

On my way out, as I was collecting my belongings at the ashram, I overheard my father. "Where is my daughter headed? Is she on the right path?" He had knelt down on a cushion in front of Babaji. My memory of that conversation, as I stood outside the door, can never be forgotten. Babaji very gently advised, "Your daughter is not wrong in what she seeks. Please take care."

It is said by a wise man that there are infinite ways of taking the journey to your higher or divine self. "If you are sincere in what you seek, it will find you."

Press Conference picture for *Chandrahas.*

Photo shoot with actor/producer Harinath Policherla.

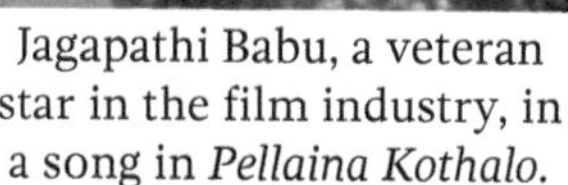

Jagapathi Babu, a veteran star in the film industry, in a song in *Pellaina Kothalo.*

I played the lead title role of Apsara in *Chandrahas.*

Dancing with live musicians and my guru, Harish Gangani, playing the pakhawaj.

Sancarana or silent movements interpreted in dance."

Nayika or heroine adorning herself.

With my guru, Harish Gangani.

Osho Buddha Purnima Festival.

Haridas Sammaroh Dance Festival in Vrindavan.

Late Swami Sevak Charan Babaji.

Playing the role of Radha with Anuj Mishra as Krishna."

Section 3

Kathak – Art of Storytelling

"When you love doing something,
do it with passion, wholly and totally."

My guru, Shri Harish Gangani, taught me dance full-time when I stepped away from my career in Telugu movies. *I believe it was my desire that was being fulfilled.* He was the younger brother of Pt. Rajendra Gangani who was assigned the title of torch-bearer of the Jaipur gharana after their father, Pt. Kundanlal Gangani, passed away. Both the brothers had handsome features and striking similarities, and I enjoyed watching them dance on several occasions at the Kamani Auditorium in New Delhi.

When I would sit down to tie my ghungroos in front of guruji, I would start feeling nervous. He would stand in front of me as my feet started moving to a particular rhythm he had just taught me. I would follow that up with my hand movements which would move in synchronization with my feet. Once he was satisfied that I had picked up a rhythm, he would sit down to play the *pakhawaj*, a classical North Indian drum. The energy in the room was captivating.

I would first recite the *bol* or *tukda* – the rhythmic syllables of dance in the counting system, in the style that he had taught me, and then follow with the dance steps. The recitation, or the speaking of the *bol*, is called *padhant* which is an important part of the dance.

When my guru would see how much I was enjoying the movements and the expressions of the dance, he would remark, "*Astha hai, to dance hai*!" In other words saying, "Where there is Astha, there is dance." Initially, it made me giggle. Once in a while he would come up from behind me and tap me on my shoulder. That was his way of saying that I was performing well.

As a side note, when I was born, my name was given to me by a priest. I was amazed to know it means 'faith'.

After at least two hours of consistent footwork and hand movements to the sound of ghungroos and the pakhawaj, I would sit on the floor next to guruji, the rhythm still reverberating in my head. Part of the flour dough that he had applied on both heads of the pakhawaj to attain the right sound would have by then rubbed off on his hands. "How do you feel now?" he would ask, as I took my ghungroos off. "Exhilarated," I would instantly reply, smiling as I wiped the sweat from my face. There were times when we would dance for five hours at a stretch.

What Harish Gangani meant to me in plain terms is… … It cannot be explained without understanding the philosophy behind the guru-shishya Parampara.

Harishji informed me that Kathak had originated from the ancient temples of North India. I immediately checked Google to read more on the history of this classical dance form for my own learning. In ancient India, performing artistes who told a story in the dance form were called Kathakars or storytellers. The word 'kathak' comes from the word 'katha' which means 'story'. Thus, I understood the origins of the Kathak dance form. Over time as I learnt the steps and movements which became second nature to me, I became engrossed with the technicalities of footwork and subtler nuances and progressed towards the finer storytelling aspects of the dance.

After three to four years of riyaz with my guru, he recommended that I join the Repertory Company of the Ministry of Culture in India. I was very nervous before the audition. "Just be confident and follow what I have taught you," he said. At the audition I performed to the best of my ability following which, some days later, I received an offer letter to join as a dancer. The Kathak Kendra Repertory is a pride of the Ministry of Culture. The Kathak Kendra was located close to Kamani Auditorium in the Mandi House area, the cultural hub of New Delhi.

Initially, being a new dancer in the team, I was uncomfortable, but I soon started feeling more confident. My trials during the few years at the Repertory Company and my time spent there are worth recalling…

On the first day, I enter the office looking bright and cheerful in my Anarkali outfit with my ghungroos in my bag. A group of boys and girls stop their work, look at me for a moment, and go back to their conversation. Someone sitting on a couch is describing a scene from a movie. The rest are hunched over that person. I take a seat.

They continue talking, and in the midst of their discussion I catch some of them looking at me. Once they are done they go into the hall adjacent to the office. In that moment I feel like a novice. I forget my background and all the experiences I have collected and feel like it is my first day at school again.

Suddenly one of them comes running towards me from the hall, giving me a look of amazement. "Oh... you must be the new dancer." She takes me inside the hall that is pleasantly large with a dance floor in the centre. On one side of the hall is the seat of the guru and next to that is where the musicians sit. The other dancers are all gathered around for their warm-up. Amongst them is Vidha Lal who in teen taal – a rhythmic pattern of a count of sixteen – is counting the beats and moving her feet in synchronization. A taal measures musical time in Indian classical music. Someone is practicing her Kathak chakkars, or spins, and one girl is practicing her hand movements. The girl who brought me inside shows me where to keep my belongings near a wall. Later, this same girl extended herself in helping me adjust my routine to the group. I realized one can go much further in life by helping others along the way. I quickly wear my ghungroos and join the others on the dance floor. I start reciting my bol loudly and follow with my footwork. The collective sound of the ghungroos is high as it resounds in the hall.

As we are warming up, a tall lady dressed in a neatly-pleated traditional Jaipur sari enters the hall. I follow everyone as they stop what they are doing and the nine of us walk up to Prerna Srimalli, our dance guru. She used to be a disciple of Pt. Kundanlal Gangani and is known for her great rhythmic talent and technique in dance. She greets everyone and starts talking about our next production. "We are going to show the nine planets in our Solar System," she says as she looks around. Her eyes come to rest on me. She at once selects me to go into the centre line with four other girls who are already in position as different planets. We begin the whole piece on the dance floor. Round and round I go, being the seventh planet. But I have no time to think of planetary positions as I try my best to learn my part in the choreography on that first day.

Into the second week of practice, I slowly start getting accustomed to my new schedule at Kathak Kendra. Along with the daily rehearsals, the dancers develop a strong sense of discipline. During our final rehearsal, the dancers spin out of control as we approach the final pose at the end of the sequence. "Be still, this is the climax!" shouts our guru from the front while we are holding our poses. She comes around to fix our positions. One of the boys has to change his place in the group to keep all the planets in their elliptical orbit. "That was ok for the first take. Now let's take it from the top," directs Prernaji. We take a break. By the end of the second week I breathe a sigh of relief as I have managed to finally grasp my part. We are now ready for our performance.

I continue my riyaz and I am happy with my routine. In my fourth week at the Kendra, as I enter the rehearsal hall one day, I see that everyone is already into their warm-up. I tie my ghungroos and quickly join the group. I assume my position on the floor, and just as I am about to practice my spins, I notice Gitanjali Lal arrive at the door. She is our new chief. She greets us warmly as we sit around her and introduce ourselves.

She calls us to the floor. The boys create an interesting montage of Lord Shiva while the girls enter from the side, right behind them, in poses that complement them. The beat we pick is on the sixth count of the beat pattern. I enter the floor on my cue. Each rehearsal feels like a performance and the adrenaline rises high.

Gitanjali Lal composes elaborate choreographies. It allows me to bring additional flexibility and range into my dance. The musical compositions are in different and new beat patterns and ragas ranging from raga darbari to raga malkauns. A raga is a series of musical notes based on different moods for different times of a day.

One day, one of the dancers asks, "Can you teach us something on Bal Krishna?" Immediately Gitanjali gets on her feet and shows us the mudras, the symbolic hand gestures, appropriate to a poem on Lord Krishna. We follow along.

On one occasion, Gitanjali tells the musicians to compose a particular piece along with her. I watch the whole composition without missing a beat. She picks up the music at the beginning and weaves our steps around a beat pattern leading to a poetic piece on Lord Krishna. It looks effortless. "Pick up on this beat in taal roopak," she tells our sarangi expert. He starts playing a melody on his string instrument. She instantly creates a dance pattern on that beat and gestures to our tabla expert who also starts playing the same pattern on his percussion instrument. She claps her hand and the dancers begin reciting the bol along with her. Finally, she creates the movements in synchronization with the music. Our poetic gestures in step with the rhythm, together with the music, fill the room with a beautiful feeling. One by one she continues to show each of us the movements, and we follow her steps all at the same time. Like this we arrive at sam, the final pose.

After the elaborate introduction, the poetry of the piece begins. The expressions, called abhinaya, are delicately woven into our steps.

It is lunchtime and all the dancers begin opening their tiffin boxes with a lot of chatter. I take out my packed foil of stuffed parathas too. Everyone begins to look at what the others have brought, trying to dig into what they fancy. "Wow, your mom's pumpkin dish tastes good," says one dancer as he tries to snatch another bite. "Hey, leave some for me! What did your mom make?" It goes on. Our meal is always with the whole group of dancers, eating and laughing together. As I watch the others, it seems as if I am living the school and college days that I missed in India.

It makes me think that it is never too late to enjoy these moments of life, appreciating the simple things and the innocence amongst my colleagues of the Kathak Kendra. Some experiences that you may have missed out in life will find you at a later stage or when it is the right time. I ponder over this thought as I chew on a paratha with curd and vegetables from my lunch box.

One day, as I begin my usual routine, someone walks in through the door. Her name is Malti Shyam. She seems familiar to me and I try to recall where I have seen her earlier at the Kendra. She is wearing an elegant off-white sari with a black brocade blouse. She greets us and begins her own training programme or talim which she carries out effortlessly on one side of the dance floor. I am affected by her presence as well as her skill in dance. She is to become my guru subsequently.

Summer is approaching and the heat is already nearing thirty degrees Celsius. One Monday, I walk into the rehearsal hall late from the horrible traffic on the highway the entire way from Gurugram. I see an elderly lady sitting in the guru's seat looking highly accomplished. The dancers are sitting around her and looking up at her with awe and admiration. She is none other than our guest teacher, a stalwart of Kathak dance, Kumudini Lakhia, a choreographer and dancer from Ahmedabad. My heart skips a beat. I know her. I quickly put my bag down and join the others as she is describing just what makes the hand movements perfect in dance. Watching her in motion, I can literally imagine myself expanding out towards the sky. Her explanations are subtle yet they speak volumes about the Kathak dance form.

She finishes talking and gives us a cue to begin. It is a new choreography which is about two people handing over a tradition of dance to the next generation. Boys rush in to a powerful beat as if they are warriors. We, the girls, join them with matching energy. It is a fascinating unfolding of a legacy of dance that takes place right there in front of my eyes.

Those were defining moments of my life.

In those years, we tour many cities in India and abroad. As I recount my memories, I smile as I remember one of my trips to Bhubaneswar in Orissa. We manage to arrive there just in time for a festival. Getting off our bus, we scramble to our assigned green rooms and change into our costumes as quickly as possible. We are just in time for our entry on stage. There are thousands packed in the auditorium that has open seating. We say a quick prayer amongst ourselves and then our eyes face the audience.

The stage is filled with the brilliant colours of our costumes. We carry out our performance in the choreography beautifully while the audience claps throughout.

Towards the end of my term at the Repertory Company, the season arrives for the Kathak Mahotsav held annually at the Kamani Auditorium, usually in the last weekend of March. The roads are jammed with artistes arriving from different cities. It is attended by the faculty, the dancers and the musicians from the Kathak Kendras of the other cities, and what is most important to me, the gurus of all the centres too. We walk in through the side entrance that leads straight into our green rooms. We give a final touch to our makeup and tie our dupattas along the side of our lehengas. Our dance piece is not only going to end the festival but it is also being especially looked forward to by the younger generation of students of the Delhi Kathak Kendra. That evening, our presentation becomes one of those performances that break boundaries. It is much appreciated by everyone including our families.

The day before the Kathak Mahotsav, on 27 March, I come in three hours late, wearing my brightest Anarkali outfit with my hair tied up. Gitanjali Lal who is sitting in the office looks up from her desk. "Oh, so you've finally decided to come?" she says, glancing at the time on the clock above the desk. I try to ignore the comment. I quickly pay my respects to her and make my way into the hall.

But that is not the end of it. In the hall I find that she has replaced me in the dance with someone else. Feeling like I have been hit in the belly, I walk back into the office. I try explaining to her, without sounding like a little kid, "Didi, this year I tried to keep it a secret from my friends that it's my birthday today, but they showed up at my house.

It's not my fault." She looks at me and simply says, "It's ok. Maybe next year you'll get a chance."

I walk out of her office holding back my emotions and simply stand in my position on the floor to continue with the dance. The others are already standing in their places, ready to go. We dance the entire piece to music without stopping. She looks at us as she comes into the hall. I complete my final turn gracefully and sit on the floor with the other girls. Finally, she backs down and gives in to my performing.

After those days, I had less interactions with my guru. He avoided calling me over and I felt a growing distance. One day I visited him at his house in Gurugram. When I greeted him he looked away for a moment. He then told me he should not have sent me to the Repertory Company so soon. I left his house crying. I had not realized that he would feel that way. Sometime after that incident, I moved on and began training under someone else.

The most important lesson I learnt: **Never let anything stand in your way. Only you determine your future. You have no option but to succeed.** How you follow your passion can determine whether you succeed or not. Your commitment to your passion is the most important factor. I was taken up with the art of storytelling and its beautiful form. "When you choose something greater than yourself, you realize you are just a drop in the ocean."

Expression of My Soul

"Certain people come into our lives for the purpose of helping us express ourselves through our creative endeavours."

The lady whom I met towards the latter part of my stint at the Kathak Kendra Repertory, I refer to as Malti*di*. 'Di' being the short form of 'didi', a respectful form of address to an older sister or any other woman. I sought her blessings and asked her if she would consider having me as her student. She became my dance guru and mentor in 2010. That is when my journey as a student and performer with her began.

Malti Shyam had started learning from Pt. Birju Maharaj at a very early age when she came to Delhi. After completing her training at Kathak Kendra, she had begun teaching students. When I started training with her in the lineage referred to as the Lucknow gharana, it was a different learning experience. She focused on making my dance form better. She showed me how to make my rotations, including my wrist movements, 'as smooth as butter' as she would call it.

When she noticed that I was a little stiff, she asked me to relax my shoulders. "Move your hands away from your chest," she said over and over again as she corrected my posture. That was her style. She would watch me carefully and break each movement down till she was satisfied. Maltidi led me to become a performer on stage, ready in all the technical aspects, and she made sure that I gave special importance to my *nakhra*, the playful expression, throughout my training.

Here is one defining moment of my training with Maltidi.

In one of the productions, *Purnanava*, at the Kathak Kendra, I played the *sutradhar* – the one who narrates the story in a play. My male counterpart was a young dancer from the Jaipur gharana. When the two of us entered the stage from opposite sides, I held my ghunghat while he held his flute. In another segment, on one side of the stage, one of the dancers took a turn bending especially low from the waist. From the wings, I watched her finishing her last turn, and taking the cue, I entered the stage with a large chest of jewels. In a sitting position, one by one, I handed over my jewellery to her, sometimes bending over to tie a piece on her hands. When Maltidi took me under her wing, she explained the points that I had brushed past earlier. She remembered seeing me in that production and she now broke down the various nuances of Lord Krishna and explained it all to me. **I realized how true it is that one should always remain like a sponge, learning and absorbing everything.** She showed me a thumri on Lord Krishna. As she sat down and played a gopi with a *natkhat* or playful expression, I got absorbed in the culture and experimented with my own spins. And as I practiced on my own, *my riyaz got better with each minute and brought me closer to my own self.*

Maltidi taught me all the finer aspects of Kathak that I wished to learn. She showed me how to hold my postures while balancing on my spins. She trained me to make my movements more delicate, and each session with her brought me closer to a whole new fragrance in my dance.

It is riyaz that fine-tunes one's posture and grace. Riyaz is key to stepping onto the stage as a performer. It is no different for any dancer from any lineage in that it requires a lifetime of practice and learning that is common to all classical forms of Indian dance. It is up to the individual to make it a part of his or her lifestyle. Both the Jaipur and Lucknow gharanas taught me what I needed to know about Kathak, and today, I feel blessed to have worked with gurus from both lineages. One needs to develop ones repertoire and technique to perform and grow as an artiste.

To explain the process of *jugalbandhi*: once my tabla player begins playing the beat, I pick it up and my feet go into rhythmic tapping immediately. The vibration of the rhythm spreads all through my body as I respond to his tempo. As his fingers glide over the instrument in perfect motion, my feet seem to move on their own uncontrollably – *ta dha ta dha*. It is like teasing in our own style of classical tabla and dance as if they are an inseparable duo. The word *jugalbandhi* comes from this Indian tradition of going back and forth to provoke and match each other's performance.

We toured most of India during the various seasons that were celebrated through festivals whether as part of tourism promotions or cultural events of music and dance. Of the many experiences of dancing on stage under the tutelage of Maltidi, particularly two occasions come to mind.

We, her students, went to the temples of Khajuraho. We were invited by the Department of Culture of the Madhya Pradesh government to perform at their annual function in the month of February. The Khajuraho Dance Festival is considered one of the famous festivals of Indian classical dances and is held beside the beautiful temples located in the Chhatarpur district.

When we arrived there, we went straight to the stage which was set up in front of one of the temples. We rehearsed Maltidi's composition end to end. The production was a timeless piece on the blossoming of spring time. In the beginning of the sequence, as we presented the approaching of spring, we rocked forward and back gently, slowly building up to the mood of the coming of the season. The dancers wove in and out with the timed rhythms. It was subtle yet powerful. In the end, we raised our hands creating silhouettes on stage. The audience gave us a standing ovation. After the performance we went on stage for the bouquet. I felt elated.

The next day we went to visit the temples. Mesmerized by the wondrous sculptures, I looked around in amazement at the beautiful depiction of dancers in the friezes that lined the outer walls of the temples.

The second occasion was when we danced at a festival in Bhopal that was organized by Sanskriti Vibhag, a cultural wing under the Madhya Pradesh government. We landed at the airport in Bhopal from where we were picked up and taken to our hotel. We freshened up and wore our costumes. There were five of us in the group. Once we had a look of the stage, our anticipation built up.

Our performance at every show would begin with the organizing committee announcing our names. We would usually be fixing our dupattas or making sure our ghungroos were fastened properly till we heard our names being announced. We would excitedly get to the side wings, ready for our entry. Finally, the music would start.

That evening in Bhopal, the stage shone with the festival sign, and the back-lit trees along the sides of the stage set the ambience for our performance. We entered with our spins. The sound of our ghungroos rang out on our rotations and we could feel the audience immediately light up. They clapped along and cheered every time we hit a sam. As I danced, I could see my guru enter from the side and take her spins. She spun faster and faster as all of us danced around her, covering the entire stage just as we had rehearsed a hundred times. We finished to a standing ovation.

During that time, one day Yamika, my guru's youngest student, told me that Maltidi was considering an invitation to perform out of the country. It was in the city of Prague in the Czech Republic. I thought it would be a great opportunity for me to perform with my guru in Europe. The trip happened in the summer of 2012. Yamika also joined us on that tour.

It was not long before I began to take up projects on my own while still under the able guidance of Maltidi. The chapter head of SPIC MACAY (Society for the Promotion of Indian Classical Music And Culture Amongst Youth) in Rajasthan, invited me to conduct workshops near the city of Kota.

I was also invited to Bahrain by the wife of the Indian ambassador there to perform at a cultural event. It was part of a special occasion that was held in honour of the ambassador. Yamika and a few other dancers accompanied me.

From then on, my performance reflected my training with Maltidi and my own dedication. I performed on several platforms across India. My family was happy to see me focused on my dance.

Whenever I think of what I love most about dance, I feel it is the poetry expressed through the gestures.

I wondered what to perform next. I asked Maltidi if I could dance to the poetry of Sufi mystics such as Amir Khusrau and Bulleh Shah. She instantly agreed and took up the idea with me. Through the next months we came up with new dance compositions. Sufi poetry began to lend a new presentation style to my dance and I travelled to several locations to perform to those pieces. My dream of dancing to Sufi poetry came to fruition.

I went to the United States and performed in Los Angeles and San Diego. The recognition that I received from my peers and other dancers in LA brought a lot of encouragement for me on my path.

At the Dharwad Utsav in Karnataka, I took along in my team hereditary professional musicians, called Manganiars, from parts of Rajasthan. I combined Kathak with Sufi whirling and we spun on stage effortlessly. The audience that stretched out in front of the stage clapped throughout, encouraging us in our performance. The show was a tremendous success due to the efforts of my team as well that worked in harmony.

On occasion I had the opportunity to visit different places to teach. Every winter I would head to Goa. I would clear my schedule ahead of time so that I could spend a few months in the coastal city. I had my lodging in North Goa where the Portuguese had once settled in various parts. The culture they left behind is reflected in the life of the city that has a mixed Goan and European culture that distinguishes itself in the world. The sunset from the beaches in Goa has a particular quality that makes seekers aware of their own being. It attracts people from all over the world, especially during the winter months. That time I was in Goa for a second visit in the same year.

I met a beautiful Russian girl who was the organizer of a dance school, Apsara School. She always got in touch with me in advance to arrange my stay. She waved at me from the distance as I went closer to her on the beach. We sat on her balcony and discussed how we could take her students forward through their next few weeks. The next day I arrived at her dance school and started with the introduction to my classes. Afterwards, the organizer and I sat out on a beautiful terrace for lunch. A bit overwhelmed by my packed schedule, I slept early that evening in spite of the loud sound of the crashing waves outside my bedroom window. The next morning I was ready to dance with the girls. The organizer and I walked together to her school.

The girls came to class with a look of excitement on their faces. A Russian translator was in the group. I walked them through all the movements of Kathak, pausing in the middle of my explanation for the translator to catch up. The girls were gathered in a circle and they listened intently. Then I began taking them through the basic hand movements and foot patterns, one by one, asking if they had any question. They listened carefully and followed along.

The sessions went as planned and we quickly overcame the language barrier. On the fifth day I started a dance choreography. I had them dance on rasika poetry from Vrindavan. I formed two groups. One sat on the floor while the girls in the other group adorned themselves as Radha. Then the groups changed sides. To conclude, both came together in a finale.

At the end of the term, the school hosted a special evening of performances under the stars in their beautiful location. The students carried out what they had learnt in the previous weeks. The audience sat in silence and watched as I led the group into a sequence of moves with their hands, then their individual dance pieces, and then the poetry on Radha.

Afterwards, my students came up to me and appreciated my efforts in coming all the way to Goa. I was extremely happy to see their excitement as otherwise it was very difficult to ascertain whether my training was reaching out to my students. Goa became a regular destination for me year after year. It was also a wonderful place to be in in the winters, away from the cold weather conditions of Delhi.

As I stood on the balcony of my room during sunset, the evening before my departure, I watched the tiny silver lining of a wave as it retreated into the ocean. Yet another year had passed. I felt fulfilment in sharing my culture with students of dance around the world.

One after another, events kept coming. I got used to being on tour four to six months in a year for various performances as well as for my teaching at different locations. I had stepped up in my game as a performer.

Those years set the foundation for my career as a performing artiste, and as I performed more frequently, the effortless pace of my life was noticed by other dancers. What my gurus taught me was essential in my learning curve and, perhaps, no one else could have given me what they did.

The essence of the guru-shishya parampara has been an integral part of the education system in Indian culture. It signifies an intrinsic bond between the teacher and the student. It can be said: *The guru is one who leads the student from darkness to light.*

But to note: **though the guru lights the path for you, it is up to you to determine how you walk on it.**

Lucknow and Sufi Influence

"Let the beauty of what you love be what you do."

– Rumi

I made my entry through the central courtyard of his bungalow into the living room. Flowing fountain water shone through the glass windows. Muzaffar Ali came down the steps with a glow in his eyes. I greeted him and we chatted about our creative projects in which he wanted me to dance. As we discussed the theme of the festival coming up in the next year, I decided in my mind how I would give it the best composition of steps, choreography and movement.

Jahan-e-Khusrau

The focus of the Rumi Foundation is to bring communities together based on mutual love and understanding, and it does this through its projects aimed to preserve the arts in society. It has been carrying forward its mission through its cultural events and festivals that are held at heritage locations. The annual Sufi music festival, Jahan-e-Khusrau, held every year in Delhi, Lucknow and various other cities, is one of its landmark activities. The festival presents artistes from different countries who bring with them distinct features of their cultures through their performances.

It all started the year before when I watched the singer from Pakistan, Abida Parveen, enthrall and uplift the audience with her Sufi songs. Being a performer, I had witnessed the festival live several times at the Humayun's Tomb site in Delhi and held a desire to meet the curator and director of the event, Muzaffar Ali. He is a filmmaker and artist and also the executive director of the Rumi Foundation. He invited me to perform at his festival the next year.

Jahan-e-Khusrau was a landmark in my performance career. In the year of my first presentation in 2013, Muzaffar Sahab chose poet Nazir for the theme of our piece. I was on stage in a duo performance with folk singer, Malini Awasthi. Smoke blew from the production set as I stood in the light waiting for my musical cue. When I went on stage, I could hear my heart pounding. I was frozen still under the glaring colourful stage lights showered on me. For a moment my eyes were blinded and then all I could see were a thousand eyes on me while I stood still in my pose. The momentary silence, that pause before the performance began, was very profound and moving. The layers of the music were carried by the light breeze and I could hear the vocal notes distinctly. Once the tabla artiste started playing his rhythmic beat, my feet began to move as if by magic.

The walls of Humayun's Tomb rose all around as I twirled to the lyrics of Nazir and the voice of Malini Awasthi. The appreciation and applause came right as I got off the stage. Long after I had finished, I still felt exhilarated from the dance.

Tea was served backstage and the artistes mingled with each other. Those are memories that will remain etched in my mind.

The next day we flew to Lucknow for a repeat performance and checked in at a hotel near Dilkusha Palace, the venue of the show. The city of Lucknow, known for its cultural heritage, is the traditional capital of Awadh, a region in the northeastern part of modern-day Uttar Pradesh.

It was like a dream. The ruins of Dilkusha Palace formed our stage backdrop and the venue was stunningly lit with magenta lights shown on the structured walls of the palace. Though the festival was similar to the one in Delhi, yet it was a different experience altogether. *I lost track of time on stage. All I remember is my ghunghat in my hand and my lehenga twirling around with me.* We were congratulated backstage by Muzaffar Sahab for a job well done.

A few months later the festival was held in Jaipur. I was always a bit nervous when an event approached because the entire choreography that I was to teach my dancers would be running in the back of my mind. My dancers, on the other hand, always enjoyed our rehearsals. Once at my studio, I was hurrying to finish the choreography of the entire piece on that day itself when Shweta said to me, "Oh Didi! Let me feel the expression of Krishna's eyes on me as I sit down." She was so engrossed in her movements that I laughed out loud, thankful for her reminder to stay calm. Needless to say, my dancers were always by my side – rehearsal onwards till the very end of any festival.

It is never easy to begin performing on one's own as a solo artiste. What makes it worthwhile is the connections one builds as well as the appreciation of the organizers of events and the audiences. The efforts of an organizing committee go hand-in-hand with an artiste's preparations to lead up to the culmination of the experience on stage.

I met Shafqat Ali Khan, a singer from Pakistan, at Jahan-e-Khusrau in 2013. In the following year, when he was coming to Delhi for a festival called Ibadat-e-Aman at the India Habitat Centre, he invited me to dance on stage with him in a collaboration. Shafqat Ali sang for the audience till late into the night. That beautiful evening of poetry and melodies remains in my heart and the hearts of those who were present.

A few months later I met Muzaffar Sahab and his wife, Meera Ali, in Gurugram. "We have a contract with the government to showcase Wajid Ali Shah in Lucknow," they said excitedly. The ballet was based on the poem "Gomti" by Rahi Masoom Raza. Its theme – a tribute to Gomti River, the lifeline and soul of Lucknow – was set in the time of the British invasion of Lucknow during the reign of Nawab Wajid Ali Shah, the eleventh and last ruler of Awadh. I felt the lyrics of the poem to be beautiful. Each line was a verse in itself. We chalked out the dances together, and I was quick to translate the pathos in the poem into movements in my dance.

In my mind I could imagine a row of dancers going down the stage with me… "Can you bring more girls?" asked Meera Ali. I immediately said yes. The show was held against the setting of the Chattar Manzil Palace, a heritage location in Lucknow. It was attended by the chief minister of Uttar Pradesh and had a packed audience that consisted largely of the residents of Lucknow.

"...as the British plundered Lucknow in 1847". the narrative goes on. A maulvi, a learned scholar, sits with a young poet amidst bodies lying on the floor. "What is happening to our country?" asks the poet. The maulvi tries to make him calm. "Don't fight, young man, against your destiny..." and he encourages the poet to express the happenings through his words.

I enter the stage, playing the character of Gomti, and enact the one-hour ballet with my dancers. Back and forth we go with the British commanders as they try to stop us, the river, from flowing. Towards the end, the soldiers capture me, Gomti, by the neck and hang me on a noose in the presence of all the villagers and townspeople who support me by calling out, "I am Gomti!"

That evening, after the performance, we had a special dinner that was hosted by a dear friend of Muzaffar Ali. She gracefully welcomed everyone into her house and served us all kinds of delicacies that I can never forget. My stay in Lucknow got extended by a few days beyond the festival and I had the privilege of attending other events organized by the foundation.

Sometime later, Muzaffar Sahab called me to his residence in Gurugram. "We are preparing for a festival to be held next February in Lucknow." "Oh. I see," I said. I loved it. It was so informal. He gave me the details. His ideas would mostly revolve around a theme to do with preserving the culture of Lucknow. We began preparing with full zest. I flew to

Lucknow for a few weeks. The ballet was called *Indrasabha* and I played the role of Sabz Pari, a celestial fairy in the court of Lord Indra.

It was a pleasure to dine with a small gathering comprising Muzaffar Sahab and his team post the success of a show. There would be laughter and conversation of how the festival had gone. Sometimes we would even discuss improvements for the next show. One time we were at Muzaffar Sahab's house in Lucknow when a young girl came to meet him. She was writing a book on Lucknow and the Awadh culture. He talked to her about his background with a lot of fervour, so I observed. There I realized what drew me to the Lucknow culture. Then he introduced us. She was a charming lady.

Lucknow's culture is uniquely preserved. It is rare to see anything like it in the world. People here respect their ancestry and give due reverence to their past. My association with the city and its culture kept growing. In a short time, many from Muzaffar Sahab's team were my fans and admirers. "There is no dancer like you in Lucknow," one of them said. They were generous with their compliments as this is their culture.

Truly speaking, central to Lucknow, a city known for its traditional cuisine and fine arts, is its culture of friendliness and courtesy. *The warmth and etiquette of the people here are qualities to note.*

There came a point when, one day, the phone rang and Muzaffar Sahab called me to his house in Lucknow on a day's notice. The chief minister of Uttar Pradesh was expected that evening for dinner. An assistant from the office called and explained the lyrics of a new ghazal, which he then emailed me. The ghazal ran in my head the whole morning. I arrived in Lucknow the same evening.

In 2018, I went back on stage in Delhi for another Jahan-e-Khusrau festival. Again a complex theme woven into a timeless ballet was presented by Rumi Foundation at Humayun's Tomb. Because of my tours abroad, it had been some time that I had met Meera and Muzaffar Ali. On that occasion, along with my team of dancers, I played the character of the Yamuna River. The same show was taken to Lucknow a few weeks later.

We mesmerized the audience with our dance. After the show I met Muzaffar Sahab who thanked me, as usual, with a warm compliment. *I went home feeling like there was nothing else in the world but me dancing on stage.*

Temple of Maheshwar, Maharashtra

We went to Maheshwar, the town of the Maratha warrior queen, Ahilyabai Holkar, in Maharashtra. We were there, by the Narmada River, for two days to film a documentary, *Maheshwari Silks and Textiles* for the Ministry of Textiles. We first flew to Indore and had lunch at Muzaffar Sahab's friend's house. We were relaxing when the dressmakers arrived to show us the special stitch of the Maharashtrian traditional sari for the Lavani dance. My costume did not fit well, I was disappointed. I remembered the perfect look of the sari I had seen in a Bollywood movie song. "How will we get this re-stitched in time for tomorrow's shoot?" asked Meera Ali. That evening we went to Maheshwar and stayed at the Ahilya Fort Heritage Hotel, the essence of subtle majesty.

We sat under a tree in the courtyard of the fort overlooking the Narmada as we were served all the courses of a traditional Maharashtrian meal for dinner. Our stay was hosted by the family that owned the resort. Afterwards, Meera Ali came to my room and said they had found someone who could redo my costume, so we would be able to go ahead with the shoot the next day. I was delighted. “Now you can sleep so you look fresh in the morning,” she smiled.

After breakfast we took a few casual shots around the fort and its entrance. I was adorned as a Lavani dancer in a traditional silk and cotton sari. While I was getting ready, Meera Ali came in to check on me. She told the stylist to fix the sari in a particular way on my shoulder. As she was going out she winked, “Don’t forget to wear the nose pin.” We had a good laugh. The nose pin or *nathani* being a mark of the traditional Lavani look, there was no way we were going to forget it. As the sari folds sat firmly on my shoulder, I looked in the mirror at myself adorned as a Maharashtrian doll and blushed.

While working with Muzaffar Ali Sahab, I learnt to be open in the expressions of my dance while portraying different characters. He often spent time explaining how a certain role should be portrayed. Each ballet performed with him helped me connect with something new. So as not to miss my association with both Meera and Muzaffar Ali, I embraced a great deal of learning from them. *If an artiste chooses to be humble, he or she can get many rewards in their presence.*

The right etiquette I learnt can go a long way and that was my learning from my experiences in Lucknow with Muzaffar

Ali. To give an example, I was in a solo performance at a festival in Jaipur at a later time. When the anchor called my name, I asked him to stop the music. Going up to the podium, I addressed the audience and asked their permission to present my dance. The viewers cheered me to go on and I began my show. I am grateful to the culture and etiquette of cities such as Lucknow that have taught me such politeness in my life.

Badshah's Kohi-'Noor'

"The best things in life are achieved while having fun."

Some of the most enjoyable moments of my dance career were with the director of Living Room Theatre, Sarita Vohra, who lived close to my house in Greater Kailash. One day I went over to her house and she looked at me, "Gosh, you're so pretty. I would love to have you as Noor in my upcoming production." I looked at her for a second, "Ahem, Noor?" I was curious. "In my play, she is a court dancer in Mughal Emperor Muhammad Shah's palace, his one and only heartthrob..." She went on for the next hour. I listened carefully to the plot of the screenplay she had written in a mix of Hindi and Urdu, and I enjoyed it thoroughly.

Sarita Vohra, playwright and director of *Badshah Rangila*, a historical musical, has written many plays for theatre audiences. She had earlier met me through a friend from my days at Kathak Kendra. She asked me to star as Noor, one of the lead characters in the play, and we started planning the music recording sessions over cups of tea. The musical score was recorded in a studio in New Delhi with a team of musicians from the city and a vocalist from Pakistan.

The plot of the screenplay went something like this:

Once upon a time there was an emperor named Muhammad Shah, also known as Badshah Rangila, who loved to sing, dance and write poetry. He was a favourite of all his subjects in the Red Fort area of Delhi from where the Mughals ruled in India. His people loved to talk about their esteemed *badshah*, or emperor, and tell stories amongst themselves of the palace and the people close to him. Then, a new dancer came to the palace – Noor. Badshah Rangila immediately liked her and told her to dance for the son of the great Persian ruler, Nader Shah, in a *mehfil* – a gathering held for the enjoyment of poetry, music and dance. The prince who had come to the palace to deliver a message, went home pleased. All this while, Noor was in love with a minister. Then the bloodthirsty Nader Shah, greedy for the Kohinoor diamond, attacked Delhi and caused much destruction to the Mughal palace.

On the first day of the rehearsals, I was the earliest to arrive at Sarita Vohra's house. A tall gentleman arrived next. He had a hint of a stubble and sideburns and looked intently at me. I paid little attention to him or to the others who walked in. Everyone took a seat, one by one, on the sofas around Saritaji's living room.

The role of the emperor was taken by Teekam Joshi, an award-winning actor from Delhi. I played Noor, the court dancer. Additionally, there was a colourful cast comprising members from different backgrounds, all residing in Delhi. They looked interesting in their characters, but I did not converse much with anyone. As the rehearsal began, I carried out my part and executed the dances in front of the group. Then I got up to leave.

"Oh Noor, you can't go yet," exclaimed Saritaji. "I want you to say one more dialogue in the end." I waited for the others to finish so I could play my part in the last scene. When I came to my dialogue, I bent down on the ground in front of the other actors and said confidently, in a mix of Urdu and Hindi, "Nader Shah, you have destroyed Delhi, but you cannot take this Kohinoor back with you to Persia!" I pretended to be hit by the poison and collapsed on the floor. When the scene was over, I stood up and gave a quick hug to Saritaji before leaving.

At the next rehearsal, "Oye, Jimmy…" called out one of the cast. Jimmy was an ex-wing commander whom I had not gotten a chance to talk to yet. "Did you fall asleep backstage during the last show?" I was checking my messages on my phone and tried not to listen. "So why were you watching me?" replied Jimmy, apparently. "We weren't watching you, but weren't you supposed to be doing something?" the first one replied. "What?" came Jimmy's voice. "The pretty girls in the play couldn't find their props. Where did you keep them?" They started laughing. I looked up from my phone. Jimmy had nearly fallen off his seat with his cheeks red while two other boys were rolling on the floor.

Just then the gentleman with the stubble walked in and looked at me with a lot of interest. He began asking me the usual questions. "So where are you from? Where did you learn to dance?" and so on… I replied to his questions briefly. I was still getting used to the environment and was yet to feel involved in the new theatre group.

Badshah Rangila was presented at the Shri Ram Centre for Performing Arts and also the India Habitat Centre in New Delhi. In the next two weeks, five more shows were held in various parts of the city. It attracted packed audiences. The one held at Epicentre, Gurugram's cultural hub, was special for me. On the closing night of the play my parents brought with them many of our relatives to see me dance in the epic role of Noor.

"Take me with you," says Noor to her lover as they meet in secrecy outside the court in the evening. He looks down and then looks up at her, "I can't Noor. please stay away from me." He remembers his duty as a minister to the emperor. She is upset and refuses to listen to his reasoning. Noor then complains to her bai, the attendant, and tells the woman that she will not back down as she loves the minister. The bai scolds her and advises her to stop thinking about him. She tells Noor to wear her ghungroos immediately as the emperor has called for her.

I remember carrying out that scene with a lot of enjoyment.

Sarita Vohra and I were in her living room when she, very passionate about the topic on which she had chosen to write her play, began telling me how the Persian ruler attacked Delhi right in the middle of Muhammad Shah's reign and took back with him generations of wealth. "But he couldn't take you with him..." She looked at me adoringly as she gave me a warm hug. She then made a gesture with her outstretched hands, almost as if she could see the wicked Nader Shah approaching in the distance, and her eyes opened wide. "*Dilli bahut door hai...*"

she said, imitating the emperor's dialogue in the play, meaning to say, "Delhi is far away…"

That was how she would narrate the play in her living room. I was transported to the court of the emperor as Saritaji continued talking: "His music composers, Adarang and Sadarang were given the royal privilege of sitting next to the emperor in the Mughal court. The court also welcomed poet Mir Taqi Mir and other musicians. The emperor himself loved dance and was a patron of the arts. The name Badshah Rangila was given to him because he valued his dancers and musicians." Suddenly, the doorbell rang.

I had made myself cozy against the cushions on her sofa while I listened to her. Someone walked in. He sat on the sofa next to me. "Saritaji, I have finally procured the costumes for the next show at the Kamani theatre." He looked like he had been running around as sweat dripped from his forehead.

"Don't tell me!" she exclaimed. "Can I get you a cup of tea?" That was her way of showing her gratitude to him. We both sat there as she went into the kitchen. "So how are you Asthaji?" asked the young gentleman. I had gotten used to seeing the people from Saritaji's team who worked closely with her. "I am well," I responded. The three of us sat there talking as we had our tea.

Kamani Auditorium was packed on that evening in September 2016. I was backstage getting my makeup done. A young boy looked at my reflection in the mirror. He was dressed like a lady. "Aye hai!" he exclaimed and clapped his hands. He had the tone of a eunuch and it struck me that that was his part in the play. "*Humme bhi thodi si apni ada sikha do*," he said seductively, which could be translated to, "Aha!

Teach me some of your nuances too." Without disturbing the stylist who was doing my hair, I looked at him and raised my hand in a *salaami*, a salute. He nearly fell from his chair while the other artistes burst out laughing.

Our entire cast gathered together before the play to say a collective prayer.

The play opens with the Azan, the Islamic call to prayer. "Delhi was the capital of the Mughal dynasty that lasted well over two centuries..." came a voice on the speakers. It is a regular day inside the court where the play begins. The ministers are congregated in front of their emperor.

We, the dancers, wait backstage for our cue to enter. We check our costumes because sometimes there are malfunctions or other mishaps: a hook on someone's dress had come unfastened, requiring us to rush and fix it before our entry. When we hear the girls from the previous act getting off the stage, we quickly wear our ghungroos for our first dance. We look at each other and feel as if we are actually dancing in Muhammad Shah's court. It is uncanny, as if it is happening again.

We enter the stage where a few actors are present from the previous scene. The hall is filled with spectators. Our first dance is on the theme of Holi, and it symbolizes the spirit of the colourful festival that was celebrated each year with zest during Muhammad Shah's reign.

At the end of the dance, Muhammad Shah takes my hand and spins me around him, admiring the way I look.

Before the next dance, I meet the minister. It is a piece based on raga malhar, the raga for the monsoon season. Then music fills the auditorium as we dance to a song set to the lyrics of Muhammad Shah. The piece is beautifully sung by well-known Vidya Shah. After the dance, there is a moment of silence as the emperor holds me close to him. I am the centre of attention in the play and loving every moment of it.

The play continues and the dancers go back on stage, entering from different corners. We hold different poses for the mehfil scene. Our positions are marked with a salaami, the royal salute to the emperor.

The emperor talks to the prince of Persia and I watch carefully from one of the archways. The minister walks onto the stage, and as I try to follow him, the emperor intercepts and takes me by the hand, closing that particular scene.

When the ruler of Persia comes to embrace Noor, she snubs him with a comment. After that she appears in the court choking, only to fall down before taking her last breath. She has just taken poison in her room. It means defeat for Nader Shah. The might of his sword could defeat the throne and take back generations of wealth of the Mughal Empire, yet he could not take this Kohinoor back with him.

Before the final scene of the play, Muhammad Shah holds me, Noor, in his lap with a look of shame and defeat. The courtesans who are crying are quickly sent away. The emperor weeps over Noor's dead body.

The play closes with the court poet, Mir Taqi Mir, conferring the title of Badshah Rangila to Muhammad Shah to honour him for keeping alive the traditions of music and dance in his court.

Mir Taqi Mir was one of the most read and respected poets of the Mughal era. The character was played by a well known theatre actor, Swadesh Mahan.

We performed the musical at several locations in India. Some of our best performances were at the Taj Mahotsav in Agra, the Indian Council for Cultural Relations in New Delhi, the Delhi Literature Festival at the Hardyal Library, and the performance at the Civil Services Officers' Institute.

In 2019, I returned to the much loved set of *Badshah Rangila* for one more performance – in Shimla.

I entered the same living room where the rehearsals used to take place. There were many new faces along with some familiar ones from our first season. Much to my relief, Teekam Joshi was there to take his highly adored and respected role as the emperor once again. I was there with a team of new dancers.

"Saritaji, we are really enjoying ourselves," said one fine lady whom I had never met before. "Let's take it up to the terrace." As earlier, a cool breeze blew from all sides. The terrace was large enough to accommodate the entire cast and crew. We had a fun time at the rehearsals with everyone laughing and enjoying their parts thoroughly. The new members were a delightful addition to the team. I slowly got to know everyone and began appreciating their pranks.

We set off for the hills in Shimla where the show was to be held at the Gaiety Theatre. The travel by road was special. In our car, a boy in the back seat started singing out loud and dancing. The person next to him, a veteran theatre actress, joined in. Next, I started dancing in my seat. Jimmy who was driving, looked at me beside him and at the others through the rearview mirror, and he burst out laughing. Poor Jimmy, he had a hard time focusing on holding the wheel steady without being distracted as the car whizzed through the mountains.

I will always remember and cherish my moments at the theatre. Set in its old-world charm, in its Gothic-style of architecture, Gaiety Theatre is located on The Ridge, which is a significant spot for tourists. The play, with its mix of dance, music and dialogue, appealed to the Shimla audience as well.

There is one incident that happened in my days with Living Room Theatre. My friend Isaah from Los Angeles watched *Badshah Rangila* at the Taj Mahotsav in Agra. After the show, he said to me, “Be humble and grounded. Don’t forget that you are here to share in your culture with your people.” I really appreciated his words. The next day, I accompanied him on his visit to the Taj Mahal.

What I took from meeting Isaah and all my theatre experiences: Do not underestimate the power of God in each one of us. **Those who are down-to-earth will be able to deal with the obstacles that come with life.**

Journey to the Middle East

"Do the things that inspire you to be greater in life."

During the last trip that I took with my ex-husband to Jordan and Lebanon, we attended a friend's wedding. Through the groom I met a lovely young lady, Alissar. One day, while I was at home in Gurugram, I received an email from her. She represented Caracalla Dance Theatre based in Lebanon in the Middle East. Alissar wanted to commission new dancers for a dance production in the Baalbeck International Festival which is the oldest and most prestigious cultural event in the Middle East.

Along with my female lead vocalist and musicians, I took a flight to Beirut, the capital city of Lebanon. We were warmly welcomed by the Arabs and given accommodation in a comfortable hotel near the Ivoire Theatre that belongs to the Caracalla group. On my first day at the Ivoire, because of the enthusiasm of Abdel-Halim Caracalla, I was compelled to put on my ghungroos and start dancing. He and his team watched me perform. Mr Caracalla is the founder and artistic director of the dance company, Caracalla Dance Theatre. His daughter, Alissar, is a dance instructor, choreographer and art director.

The next morning we drove for two hours to their recording location. As we went up a mountain, on the way we got to see what a small country Lebanon is as it stretches along the eastern shore of the Mediterranean Sea. We spent nearly seven hours recording our music in the studio that day.

We met a fine music composer from Iran whom we called the music maestro. In spite of his humble and down-to-earth nature, we could gauge that he had sound experience and excellence in the international music industry. We were excited to be working with him.

I headed back to India with my team. As part of our agreement, I had to round up my dancers. I spent the next three months organizing my team in Delhi for the festival which was to celebrate its sixtieth anniversary in 2016. We were back in Lebanon three weeks before the date to join the Caracalla dancers for our combined rehearsals. The feel of the preparation during those weeks was similar to that of my corporate days in America: long durations of practice sessions at the venue and limited time in the hotel where we went back only to sleep. My dancers were not used to it, but all of us adjusted.

The grounds of the festival, a two-thousand-year-old Roman temple site, were nothing like we could ever have imagined. The Temple of Bacchus, in the Baalbek city temple complex, held our stage that was erected towards its front steps. The walls of the temple rose all around us as we walked amidst the ruins. My heart fluttered for the tenth time on the first day as I turned yet another corner and looked at a different set of ruins from the past. The ancient site was what one would imagine to be the set of a period movie. In fact, when my dancers and I roamed about the ruins, we could indeed feel as if we were walking in the midst of the remains of one of the oldest places in the world.

It is a site of much significance and I had never even heard of it. We had gone from India to perform at such an important location without knowing anything about the history or culture of Lebanon. Thanks to my subsequent visits to that amazing country and the numerous friendships that I cultivated there, I have finally understood the importance of Lebanon and its ancient temple site.

My dancers were initially excited about the new diet, which they got used to and also tired of within a week. "Put that thing on top of the pita bread and eat it." I heard one of them say to another during breakfast at our hotel. The buffet spread had the usual haloumi cheese platter along with the salads and the hummus. My dancers helped each other a lot during that tour as most of them were completely new to the environment, having travelled to that part of the world for the first time.

It was the opening night of the production *Sailing the Silk Road*. We quickly put the finishing touches to our new costumes. We could feel the anticipation building for the show. *Nothing can describe the experience that we went through in those moments as we stood behind the stage that was set up for the production.* We peeked from behind the set and saw the large audience stretched out in the front, eagerly waiting for the performance to begin. It was intimidating. On the other side of the set, the darkness of the ruins seemed to entrap us in another time. *It was as though we were standing between two worlds*. We were depending on our performance to go as we had rehearsed in the previous weeks. And it did! The act mirrored the time on the Silk Road. Each country shone like a mirage, depicting its significant monuments along with its culture of music and dance.

Our next tour with the same company for the same production was at the Royal Opera House in Oman. Soon we were busy preparing for that show.

We were at my new studio in Greater Kailash. A fresh set of dancers was added to my older group. “We are going on another important tour,” I told them, “I want all of you to give your best.” As soon as I finished speaking, two of the dancers put on their ghungroos and stood up. Three times we rehearsed the entire piece that we had performed at the Baalbeck International Festival, pausing in between only to make minor adjustments. My regrouped team of dancers accompanied me to Oman and also to my future trips to Lebanon.

The Royal Opera House in Muscat

The city of Muscat was like a piece of art painted by Sultan Qaboos, the Sultan of Oman at that time. He had transformed it. Muscat is the perfect city with its wide roads, its large mosques and its white buildings engraved with Arabic calligraphy. The beautiful white marble dome of the Royal Opera House stands in the heart of the city, a symbol of pride for the people of Oman.

The gesture of the Caracalla dance company, of inviting us to join their dancers on their tour of Oman, was enough of a welcome for us. We were exhausted from our long flight but went straight for our rehearsal. As we entered the auditorium, we gasped in astonishment at the architecture and design. We stood on the stage overlooking the rows of red velvet seats and gaped in awe at the high ceiling above us. The engineers were busy setting up the stage truss for the lighting equipment. We went to our green room. The large corridors outside the auditorium were like a maze.

The first show of *Sailing the Silk Road* was held at the Royal Opera House in the presence of distinguished guests of the royal family, the media and the general public. The previous days of back-to-back rehearsals had given us very little time to rest. Finally, after the first show, we breathed a sigh of relief.

As I went in and out of the auditorium, I saw the charming Mr Caracalla who greeted me with a nod. He was correcting the postures of dancers and incorporating changes after the first show of the previous evening. According to some of his students, Caracalla Dance Theatre was every dancer's dream, and Mr Caracalla was often seen promoting the dance and culture of Lebanon through the media. I had gotten used to seeing their zeal in the eyes of the Caracalla dancers. They were dedicated and believed fully in what they were doing with their talent.

We returned to Delhi. We had gotten used to working with one of the best companies in the Middle East in their unique oriental style of dance. Their manner of communicating, with the warmth and professionalism so natural to their culture, had rubbed off on us. "Habibi! We were so happy to go on that tour Didi!" exclaimed Mayukh with a smile. "Habibi!" I expressed my agreement with him.

A few months later, “How are you, Habibi? We have another proposal for you,” came the voice of Mr Caracalla’s secretary on the phone. As usual she spoke with a lovely accent. “We are going to invite you to Beirut again.” I hung up the phone and shared the good news with my family. “I’m going on tour to Beirut, the Paris of the East, to perform,” and I followed it with, “for three months!”

Everyone was amazed at the news. I flew to Beirut alone to discuss and finalize all the details of the contract. On my return, two new dancers joined my group.

My dancers were excited but equally apprehensive regarding how they would take time off from their regular jobs and other activities. The next two months were filled with anxiety as they asked me all sorts of questions related to their stay in Beirut: the accommodation, rehearsals, the food, and so on. I went back and forth with Mr Caracalla’s secretary to answer all those questions. Finally, the day arrived for us to head to Lebanon.

Three Months of Performing in Beirut

Our production was to open at the Forum de Beirut, an events venue, officially for the public. At the Ivoire we blended well with the other groups from various countries. We enjoyed watching the Caracalla dancers rehearse their sequence on stage and perfect their routine. My dancers and I soon became part of the whole set-up, quickly picking up speed and incorporating the changes told to us into our routine.

We were finally ready for the opening night at the Forum de Beirut. We could hear the audience taking their seats, and then the pin drop silence. Our ghungroo bells tinkled backstage in the green room. The set was a mirror image of the structure of the Temple where we had performed earlier. The show lasted for almost two hours. It was an enthralling experience for us. We could feel the forum come alive with all the dancers going back and forth between the auditorium and the backstage areas. It felt like the movie *Gladiator* with all its special effects.

My solo entry felt different each time. I kept my dance form very close to the tradition as I was taught in India. The time came for my group to enter. The ten of us executed on the beat the sharp twists and turns of our Kathak set to the pure syllables of the dance style. Next, we welcomed the sailors on the set as part of our routine. Then all of us came together with the other dancers for a grand finale. *Each time on stage was not only a new experience but we also pushed our boundaries.*

For a scene in Venice, the one performed just before ours, we cleared a side wing completely for a group of boys and girls to pass through unhindered. We watched as the boys lifted the young damsels on their shoulders and entered the stage. They spun around in unison and ended with a sharp turn and a clean bow. Their hats were tipped towards each other first and then the audience before they exited. It was like their version of what I had seen at a Mardi Gras celebration in the United States. We had all learnt to seamlessly leave way for each other at the wings as we entered and exited the stage.

The costumes of the dancers of the different countries caught my attention. I noticed the striking colours in rich velvet and patterns on borders. Each country showed off its colourful costumes, ornaments and headgear.

The audience in Lebanon was delighted with the production and gave us a standing ovation for a brilliant performance. We took a curtain call together. For the entire period of three months, we had sold-out shows with packed audiences rising to applaud at the end.

It was a spectacular way to experience the Middle East. The prelude to each performance actually happened backstage when we were getting ready as a team, excited about going on stage. And each time it seemed the audience was even more enthusiastic than the previous performance. *We had never seen anything like it earlier.*

Our take-home from that experience was the environment in which we had worked. The Caracalla Dance Theatre is known for its tradition of discipline. It is its hallmark under which dancers associated with the company perform. We too got used to working in that setting. We also loved the way we went back and forth with their dancers between the acts, twirling in our own styles and techniques in a spirit of individual yet collective energy and all the time cheering each other.

The experience was a validation of our own talent and the arriving at that level of perfection that is a signature of the Caracalla style. We went on to perform with them in many other countries in the years to come.

Felicitated by Pt. Rajendra Gangani.

Spinning and striking a pose.

Rehearsal before the show in Khajuraho.

With my guru, Malti Shyam, at the Khajuraho temples.

Performing for SPIC MACAY.

Always wearing beautiful costumes by Muzaffar Ali and Meera Ali for their productions.

The team at Jahan-e-Khusrau festival.

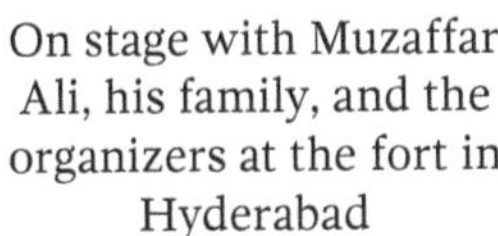
On stage with Muzaffar Ali, his family, and the organizers at the fort in Hyderabad

The cast of Badshah Rangila.

The king's court dancers

The dances during Badshah Rangila.

The emperor played by Teekam Joshi and myself as Noor.

Getting ready to go on stage."

High energy with the Caracalla team.

We performed *Sailing the Silk* Road over 50 times in 5 different countries.

Amidst the ruins of Baalbek temple complex during rehearsals.

Shopping in Kuwait before our show.

The Royal Opera House where we performed in Muscat, Oman".

We learnt to hold our poses perfectly and improve on our choreography while performing in various countries

Section 4

Dadi and My Dance Studio

"The journey ebbs and flows. For every good phase in life, there has to come a challenging one."

There was a surge of success in my performance career and the name Astha became synonymous with my dance performances. But that was also a time in my life when I went through turmoil and deep challenges. *However picturesque one's life is at any given moment, there are extreme challenges that one has to overcome.*

After the two-year renovation period of the house in Greater Kailash, I moved in. For a while I had my living-room-turned-studio to myself, and I enjoyed practicing my dance with my ghungroos on and rehearsing with my dancers and musicians. My dadi, who had moved to my parents' residence before the renovation, started insisting on returning. My parents believed that she would continue to live with them, but she was bent upon going back to her own house. No one could say anything to her. One day, soon after her return, she entered my studio in the midst of one of my rehearsals for a production and got upset at seeing the girls practicing in front of mirrors.

She walked away but later told one of them that it is not proper for a girl in our society to dance. I realized that living with my grandmother was not going to be easy.

One time, I had scheduled a workshop with my guru Malti Shyam and her students, in my studio, to expose the younger generation of dancers to her style of dancing. On the second day of the workshop we were enjoying the new learning environment and talking and laughing amongst ourselves when there too my grandmother walked in and told the girls to leave the house.

I could not understand that side to my dadi. I had heard that some people look down at dance as a career, but I was not sure if she felt the same. When I tried to talk with my parents about it, they took her side. Ever since I had begun living away from them in Greater Kailash, a gap had started to form between us. I had not realized that the conservative thinking that prevailed in society would affect them in spite of their giving me a western upbringing. From then on a series of incidents happened that led me to a realization that made me uncomfortable. *People always act in convenience with regard to their surroundings. They choose not to oppose others if it means going against the current.*

I continued to stay focused on my dance routine and my schedule of performances. It was my way of dealing with what I was facing at home. Maltidi called me to her house one day to show me an earlier performance of hers at the Old Fort in Delhi. Her dancers had gone on stage to the reverberating sound of 'Aum' and had danced with their footwork completely in synchronization with the music. Slowly, as the lights dimmed, they circled around each other a few times and arrived at the final sam. The piece was about Lord Shiva and it felt like His character had come to life. **Those moments for me were like pearls of wisdom that carried me through my journey in India.** I danced to that same piece along with my guru at various festivals. I appreciated her way of showing me her previous works to involve me in her choreographies. *By being a sponge around her in those days, I was able to absorb everything.*

My dadi was strong-willed. She did not require much assistance even though she was close to ninety years of age. She preferred not to have too many relatives visiting her. An uncle, another of my father's brothers, was around to help her when she needed. Despite our differences, my dadi and I lived together in that house for several years.

The house was very quiet. I could hear the sound of my footsteps in the afternoons when my grandmother rested in her room. It was the perfect time for dance and music. I would usually have electronic tabla beats along with raga notes playing in the background in my dance studio, and I would practice my moves to a particular rhythm. Sunlight from the central courtyard would shine into the bedrooms around it, one of which was converted into a *baithak* or lounge. It was the coziest part of the house where the family naturally got together. People visiting us mentioned that the place had a peaceful vibe. The garden in the front had been left as it was before the renovation and the place retained its earlier charm.

My mother had a reliable maid, Siya, who moved in with me to help me handle my affairs. She began taking care of the cooking and cleaning, and she even helped me pack my costumes and jewellery when I travelled for my shows.

Siya would be cooking in the kitchen when I woke up in the morning. I could hear the sound of the pots and pans as she placed them around or from one stove to another. She would ask, “Didi, your tea is ready. Shall I serve it to you outside?” She had heard my dancers address me as didi and had started doing the same. “Yes.” I loved to sit outside in the old garden. She would bring my tea made with fresh ginger, cinnamon and black pepper, the way I like it.

One morning, by the time I came out of the shower, she had my breakfast laid out on the table and my clothes neatly ironed. “Clear everything after you eat. The Khan Saabs are coming in an hour.” I address my musicians as Khan ‘Saabs’, which refers, more than anything else, to a level of creativity they have achieved. All of them are from musical backgrounds, and they have been playing for me since my days at the Kathak Kendra. We have years of experience of performing together. They accompanied me to the Baalbeck International Festival in the Middle East and, after that experience, I had decided to do something new with the same group for the upcoming Hampi Karnataka Festival.

I adjusted things around in my studio so that the cushions were neatly arranged for the musicians to sit near the wall. I turned my electronic raga machine to a soothing musical note and lit some incense. By the time the musicians arrived, my maid had cleared the kitchen and was in her room.

“Don’t be formal,” said Fateh Ali Khan as I went out to call Siya. “It’s ok Khan Saab,” I said. I had invited them in and they were seated comfortably. I knew the musicians were usually running around all day and I was interested in getting the maximum out of them. “Creating poetry with music isn’t something that happens overnight Khan Saab," I laughed. "It takes skill, passion and creativity." "Make everyone some nice tea." I told Siya.

Ahsan Ali started playing with his strings, trying out a few notes on the sarangi. Fateh Ali Khan, also on a string instrument, the *sitar*, sat quietly, waiting for us to figure out our first few notes. When he played, he tied it all together in seconds. Amaan Ali, my tabla player, then gave the best possible rhythm on his instrument. He was skilled and natural in his technique when he played in accompaniment to dancers. That was how we created our first composition. Soon we went on to the second. I had lots of ideas running through my mind. "Let's do something like this." I recited some bol patterns. We picked up a new count in a medium tempo and created a whole new structure around it with those bols. Every time, before going to the next piece, we clarified the entire structure of the composition already done. "We go to the next verse after eight counts." I coordinated with Amaan Ali on the tabla.

The tea arrived. "Thanks, please keep it here..." I told Siya who had also brought some snacks in accordance with my prior instructions. We sat there eating and discussing our next piece. After our light meal we finished a third composition, and then everyone sat back relaxing after our long rehearsal. Time just flew by.

"*Ijazat len*?" asked Ahsan Ali, politely requesting my permission to leave. "Sure," I said, "when do we meet next?" We still had one last piece to complete before the festival. "Let's meet in two days and then we can rehearse again a day before the show," replied Ahsan Ali.

In the afternoon, as I rested, in my mind I went over the patterns that we had rehearsed. In the evening I called my tabla player to give him some more patterns in the same tempo. "I'm such a music buff, even I didn't know it," I said to myself jokingly as I patted myself on the back.

"I'm going in a few days," I told Siya. "Ok, where?" she asked curiously. She loved to hear of the places my dance adventures took me to. "To Hampi. I'll be back in about a week." I appreciated her round-the-clock presence with me and I enjoyed seeing her innocent excitement.

"Didi, which costumes are you going to take with you?" she asked. I pulled out the two outfits from my closet that I was considering as well as my jewellery, makeup box, ghungroos, some clothes and miscellaneous items. "Pack these," I said, pointing in the direction of my four-wheel suitcase that had been kept aside just over a fortnight ago. Siya took care of it all. I found my clothes and everything else neatly lined up in my bag. After taking a good look around to make sure I had not left anything, I was on my way to the airport, excited about the approaching live performance with my team.

The management committee of the festival had sent someone to pick us up from the airport and take us to our hotel that was located close to the performance venue. In the hotel lobby, we met some celebrities from the music industry in Mumbai. They were as excited as us to perform for the crowds at the festival. The following morning, we drove to the temple complex. There were stages set up between the numerous temple ruins. Artistes were already performing and crowds were gathered at each stage. After driving around we stopped at a new temple site from where we could hear music playing. We walked closer to the stage and found it was one of the largest set-ups at the festival. It had a band playing to a crowd of close to a thousand people.

We took our turn on the stage. My musicians sat to my right as I stood in the centre of the platform. I fixed my eyes on the crowd and began to dance. When the audience applauded at the end of my performance, I was filled with emotion and cried from my heart. It was a beautiful feeling.

I thought: **"I know why I am here. To share my experiences with others while on stage."**

As we went down the steps of the stage, we were congratulated by the organizers as well as the next team that was to perform. I still had tears in my eyes as I was touched by the audience and the performance. But without making it obvious, I got into the car and we drove back to the hotel. The next day we took an early flight to Delhi.

It was a routine that continued for some time: my going back and forth between my studio and the different cities that I visited. I would go to my parents' house in Gurugram on the weekends when I was in Delhi. My parents had settled well in India and seemed to have left their old days in America behind. But what I could not understand was why they had started questioning me on my lifestyle and future plans. It made me uncomfortable. I could not give them a definite answer as I was busy with all the excitement of my career and enjoying my life. I felt the gap widening between us in our communication. I did not pay much attention to their worries, not that I can say I understood what they felt.

I here refer to an individual as a family friend. He met us at that time through a relative and invited us to his house for dinner. He was interested in getting to know my parents but, I think, more about my way of life, especially the time I had spent in spirituality and ashrams. He asked us awkward questions particularly about my plans and my personal life. *It was trouble at first sight.* Because of the nature of his queries, my parents began getting confused, and this person, taking advantage of the situation, suggested to them that I see a psychiatrist who happened to be a close relative of his.

When I met the psychiatrist and she spoke to me, I felt something strange. Being naive about the situation I was getting into, I agreed with her on going through some basic tests that turned out to be rather random and unconvincing. Despite the test results being inconclusive, the lady suggested to my parents that I consider getting admitted to a particular hospital so I could be kept under close monitoring. She and her husband happened to be on the board of directors of the same hospital. I was against the idea and what she suggested. A few days later, we met the same people over coffee. I was uncomfortable in their company. My bewilderment regarding what was going on convinced the family friend and the psychiatrist that I needed their help. What was worse, they even *influenced* my parents. There was no basis for their assumption. It seemed they were pushing their way into our family affair, taking advantage of my parents' concern about my marriage. I had no idea that I was going down a deep gorge.

That summer, I took a trip to Shimla hill station with my family. We rented a cottage on a road that ran parallel to the Mall Road but was lower on the mountain slope. I used to go down the slanting road and take walks by myself in the forest. The house had tall trees on one side of it and on the other there was a steep climb up to the main road. Except for the meals with my family, I was on my own for most of the time and I felt carefree to sing, dance, explore the narrow paths and take in the fresh mountain air. "Is there anything in life at all?" I would ask myself.

Midway into our vacation, my father one day exclaimed loudly, "I have a backache, I need to return to Delhi." On the drive back in the car, I could sense the awkwardness between my family and me. There were still two months left of the summer and I had nowhere in particular to be or anything to do since my tours were to resume only in August. Moreover, all my friends and dancers were on vacation and our dance sessions were at a halt. So, I continued to stay with my parents. Those two months were *very* uncomfortable. *That phase was a challenging one where I faced difficult times being alone on a chosen path.* I was used to being busy either engaged by festival organizers or in my own projects. I also had my lifestyle as a performing artiste and a dance teacher.

One morning I woke up with a headache and a dizzy feeling. I could not get out of bed. I tried to rise but felt a heavy weight on my body. I did not know whom to call, not knowing what was happening to me. I felt myself slowly slipping into some haziness and an uncertain part of my subconscious mind that I could not understand. My eyesight became foggy. I called my mother. She gave me a cold look and said something hastily. It was unlike her. My father too looked at me but did not say much. I wondered why they were not communicating properly with me. My brother was his usual self but I could not really open up to him. I started reacting to my parents' behaviour towards me and became unusually moody with them.

I called an ayurveda doctor whom I trusted. He told me to jog every morning and also advised that I focus on my diet to get back to the way I was. He said he sensed signs of depression. I made efforts to get out of bed in the mornings, but I could not. Each day things got worse. I remember standing in my parents' room and trying to dance, but I could not move my muscles.

I called Maltidi. She talked to me sweetly on the phone and then came over to meet me along with her husband. She said I must do whatever possible to prevent going any deeper into my condition and to be easy on myself. "Just throw it out of the window," she said in very simple terms. She encouraged me to dance and to lift myself out of my state through my riyaz. She and her husband said positive things about me to my parents and tried their best to lift our spirits. When they left, I felt so alone. I felt like I did not have a single soul to turn to for advice.

After a few months, I went to Vrindavan to ask Babaji if he could offer any guidance. His loving presence and concern were obvious, but, unfortunately, he could not do anything to help me sort out my problem. I met a young girl at the ashram. She accompanied me on my return to Delhi and stayed with me to see if she could offer any support. After spending a few days at Greater Kailash, we went to my parents' house. For the first time my mother came forward, "We've been giving you a medicine that you didn't know about." She did not say anything more, however, I understood. She handed me a box of quick-dissolving antidepressants or stabilizers. I was shocked but could not express my feelings to my parents. My mother tried to convince me to continue the medicine. I left their house and returned to Greater Kailash.

On my own, I felt slightly better. "At least I will be able to make my own decisions," I thought. But one day I felt like I could not go any further. I had the worst pain inside and my head constantly hurt. I visited a doctor near my house who prescribed a simple dose of antidepressants. At first I was reluctant to take the medicine. I shuffled through the drawers in my kitchen, looking for any natural herb or ayurveda medicine that could possibly help the situation, but I could not find anything. I sighed deeply. I knew I had no choice.

I had to start with a small dose of the antidepressant and that itself had a prolonged effect on me. After some time, the doctor added a sedative and then something for alertness. A short while later, I spent a week with a friend of mine at her village near the Delhi-Haryana border. The fresh countryside air and pure food made with love were healing. My friend, who had been shocked to see my state, was happy to see me better.

Some months passed and I went on my usual trip to Goa that winter. A dance school, Temple of Dance, had invited me to perform and teach at the school for two months. The place was serene and beautiful. I did my best every morning to wake up, get dressed and go to the school to teach Kathak. I could not tell anyone what I was going through. The girls came in everyday with their ghungroos and diligently listened to and followed my instructions. Many times they would ask to record the sessions for their future practices and I would give them permission to have their video cameras on while I danced and showed them the moves. They enjoyed the classes immensely and absorbed the lessons that they eventually took back with them to their countries. They were very grateful to me. There was tremendous power in teaching especially to such open and radiant people.

I was completely focused on my work, but I was so distant within myself that I could not enjoy or appreciate anything good that was happening in my life. I was not my usual self and was still continuing my medication.

It turns out that many people on the spiritual path go through a mental, physical and emotional struggle. Additionally, the life-force kundalini energy can cause worry and confusion in the mind for seekers. Doctors can only attempt to treat such people for a short term as their methods are not long-lasting and effective. After trying their medicines I realized that I was not going to find my solution in those treatments. As time passes, the energy balances out by itself.

When I went back to Delhi, my dadi started calling my parents and complaining about my living in Greater Kailash. My parents' worries got exaggerated and our relationship had its ups and downs throughout the next year. In that most difficult phase of my life, I staunchly believed I was a fighter and that I would not give up. I continued to stay in that house in Greater Kailash and tried my best to focus on my dance.

I was in the Middle East on a dance tour when I got the news that my grandmother had passed away. On my return, I immediately went to my parents' house to stay with them for some time. A few months later, I visited the Greater Kailash house. I hung some of my dadi's old artefacts on the walls to feel her presence around me. With her passing, it was the end of that generation of the family. My paternal grandfather, a highly reputable eye surgeon, had passed away many years before while we were still in America.

The lesson: Nothing can explain or make things easier, but you have to keep **trusting your intuition to follow your dreams.**

Continuing My Spiritual Growth

"But few are those who tread the sunlit path; only the pure in soul can walk in light."

– Sri Aurobindo

After my grandmother passed away, I stayed with my parents for a few months. My mother insisted on accompanying me everywhere as she did not want me to be alone. The cultural entrepreneur and founder of Utsav Music Productions in Chennai, Churchill Pandian, arranged for my visit for the annual Strings and Bells concert series at the Yagnaraman Festival. It was to be held at the Krishna Gana Sabha, one of Chennai's oldest concert halls. It is a great privilege for any artiste to perform at that location. I actually got excited and phoned my friend Deepak Pandit, a well known violinist in Mumbai who was to play a duet with me on stage. "You really are the only one who can do a duet with me for the festival," I said to him. He had happily agreed to Mr Pandian's request and had arranged for his percussionist to accompany him.

My mother took the flight with me to see my show in Chennai. Deepak and I met the next morning and we had a wonderful rehearsal on the stage of the Sabha in the presence of Mr Pandian. I then rested through the afternoon. In the evening, I was nervous. I wore my signature outfit that always shone on stage in my performances. Deepak Pandit opened the show and I made my entry on a particular twang of his violin. Amidst the rasikas of Chennai our classical jugalbandi, or duet performance, was much appreciated. My mother loved the show. The next day we went with Churchill Pandian in his car to Pondicherry, a union territory located within Tamil Nadu to the south of Chennai. It was a beautiful drive and we enjoyed the green landscapes going past us.

Pondicherry is known for its French-styled streets and cafes with a bit of the European flair. For seekers of spirituality, it is known for its Sri Aurobindo Ashram and Auroville which attract tourists throughout the year. For nature lovers too, the city offers its beaches and lakes. I looked forward to visiting Auroville with my mother and Churchill Pandian who had been there many times. As the car neared our destination, Mr Pandian asked, "Do you'll know anything about Auroville?"

"It's famous for a meditation dome," I immediately said, perking up. I had read about it and seen pictures in magazines. The car wound through the bougainvillea-lined narrow lanes that led towards Matrimandir, also known as the soul of the city, and we pulled up at the visitors' car park.

The large golden dome of Matrimandir holds spiritual significance and is a spot for seekers to meditate. Established by the Mother of the Sri Aurobindo Ashram, it is situated in the centre of a large open area with gardens called Peace.

The ambience that one steps into transports one to a heightened level of consciousness. It is a true feast for the eyes. My moments inside Matrimandir were silent and profound. We walked back through the gardens towards our car, enjoying the swaying of leaves in the breeze.

Sri Aurobindo Ashram is situated on a French-styled cobblestone street. The place is a stark contrast to life anywhere else in India. Taking particular notice of the main gate, we removed our shoes outside and entered. The ashram was filled with the scent of incense which smoked from the great big *Samadhi* – the tomb of Sri Aurobindo and the Mother. The fragrance of fresh flowers too filled the air. The tomb is set in the centre of a courtyard and there were people seated near it. I meditated for a few minutes and then we paid our respects. After taking a quick look at the university gift shop, we headed back to Chennai.

I went to Chennai to perform on multiple occasions with Churchill Pandian and other organizers. Once I was in Trivandrum for the Sai International Arts Festival. The organizer, Veena Janardhanan, greeted me with warmth and affection. She looked forward to my performance. There were other artistes who arrived too. The auditorium had a slanting roof and looked like an Indonesian hut, open on all sides. On the evening of the show, it started raining. As sheaths of water came pouring down all four sides of the auditorium, it created a magical effect. In the finale piece, I danced to the poetry of Bulleh Shah.

In spite of my personal struggles, I was able to perform at various festivals of repute during that time. I often remember the state of confusion I would be in, the night before a show, regarding what I would do the next day and how I would make my entry in front of the audience, but it always went well. **Being an artiste, there was always adrenaline. And no matter what I was going through inside, I always did my best on stage.**

Mr Pandian invited me to also perform in Hyderabad and Cochin. I arrived in Cochin. The show was held at the Bharatiya Vidya Bhawan and was supported by the Indian Council for Cultural Relations as well as the *Times of India* newspaper. After the performance, I asked Mr Pandian if I could stay an extra two nights at an ayurveda centre. It was a time of relaxation for me at the centre where I was given traditional hot oil treatments. I started feeling better with regard to all the discomfort that was going on within me. I also stopped my medication.

When I returned to Delhi, my relationship with my parents continued to be tensed. My family, though extremely proud of my achievements, was getting increasingly concerned about my being single and also about my having chosen dance as a path that had many uncertainties. I, however, felt that I had certainty about my passion and that other things would fall into place eventually.

I wanted my freedom to follow my dance and I never really argued with them, I do not know why. Maybe I did not feel the need to, knowing perfectly well that I was on my path. But they placed a lot of emphasis on my settling down and I started feeling a constant pressure building within me from their nagging.

I decided to move somewhere out of Delhi. I made a call to my friend, Fatima, in Mumbai. She was excited that I had called her after so long. I confided in her and expressed my desire to relocate. It so happened that a month later Churchill Pandian shared the good news that I would soon be performing at the National Centre for Performing Arts (NCPA) in Mumbai. The theme of the show, *Mera Shyam*, was based on Lord Krishna. It was about the women who have loved Him – during His lifetime and afterwards. I was excited about depicting Lord Krishna's consort, Radha, and happily started composing my dance piece for my performance. I enjoyed portraying the character through my mudras and timed expressions. My performance went off well and Fatima, who met me after the show, congratulated me. We sat at a restaurant nearby, casually chatting and catching up. We also talked about my move out of Delhi and about Mumbai being an option.

I returned home and told my parents about my idea to move to Mumbai. The city had a temperate climate and, compared to Delhi in those days, had a lower pollution level that I preferred. I planned to look for a place near the sea and that was a great advantage point for me in living there. I went to Mumbai and stayed at Fatima's house while I looked for a place for myself.

Once I had moved, people whom I knew began suggesting that I meet casting directors for auditions into films. It meant visiting the crowded parts of the city and sometimes going to meetings in the hope of a lead into a movie. Things had changed quite a bit since I had been in Hyderabad. However, I kept looking for any sort of a re-entry into movies through my dancing talent and auditions. I began working on a short film with one producer. A while later, a girl who had been my student on a previous tour, joined me in Mumbai and our dance classes started in my apartment. I became busy with the intricacies of the dance patterns, weaving choreography into her steps.

In the middle of the monsoon, I woke up one morning and found that my mother was calling. She insisted that I get home immediately for the celebration of an Indian festival. While I packed my bag, I looked out at the pattering rain. How was I going to like going back to the Delhi heat?

At home in Gurugram, I was at dinner with my family when I suddenly got a phone call from a dance organizer in Delhi. He requested that I meet him the next day.

The Breakthrough

"When there is a true union of the mind, body and soul, that is when life happens."

My visit to my parents' house continued for longer than I had expected. And in that time I saw how single-minded and preoccupied my parents were about my settling down. Society, seemingly, had put a pressure on them and that was where all our disagreements began. Anything I did, did not 'fit in' to their standards of me. The truth of the matter was, I became uncertain of what to do or say to them.

The cultural conditioning of my parents allowed them to be vulnerable to society. In India, it is a common occurrence that when a daughter tells her family that she is going to go out and do something different, no one openly opposes her, but it is hoped that she will come out of it and eventually settle down and shape herself into what is called a stereotypical daughter or, in some cases, a daughter-in-law.

Being extra strict, my mother told me to remain inside the gated complex of their colony and not go anywhere without telling her. "You are not allowed to leave unless it's for something urgent." I realized that that is exactly what society wants: to limit a girl's access and exposure, to silence her dreams and aspirations, so that she is forced into becoming an image of what others want her to be.

Each time I tried to reason with them or argue a point, my parents brushed me off saying that I was the one who needed readjusting. For everything I said, they said things tenfold to support their stance. In spite of my trying hard to convince them, they did not understand that I did not have a problem with my life. But that was not the difficult part. My real predicament was that while I was dealing with all those issues with them, I was also doing my best to play my part by keeping peace with everyone at home. My parents had no way of understanding that. *This is only for those to understand who are on a spiritual path and have gone through something similar. In other words, for those who have experienced a spiritual awakening. And it is for them alone to deal with in their own time.*

What further discouraged me was that my parents set me on a guilt trip regarding where I was headed in life and how I had deviated from my goal. My father had always supported me in my career at Deloitte in the United States. And, afterwards, he had also supported my interest in dance. However, at that point, it seemed they were opposed to my way of life and only wanted that I marry and settle down like everyone else in our society. *There is a societal pressure one has to deal with especially in India*. I had to deal with my parents' fears regarding what they believed they were facing – the stigma and judgement of their peers and society. And, simultaneously, I was trying to live my own life. I did not wish to deal with anything or anyone while I was going through those problems with my family.

I went to Mumbai to finish my short film, but decided to move back to Delhi to focus on myself.

I spent that period of my life thinking of how to take my life forward. "God, where is this going to head now?" I would pray. When my parents would confront me on any matter, I would go into my room and shut the door. **Turning on loud music, I would dance like an Indian Goddess in front of my mirror. Seeing myself in the mirror gave me courage and strength to be who I was – a symbol of hope for myself and others. I had to fight for my right to exist without being judged.** Sometimes I would put on my headphones and speak gibberish out loud. After some minutes of that, I would finally hear silence. One afternoon I was browsing through channels on television. The entrance door opened and my mother walked in. She saw that I was in my place, doing what she thought I should be doing. Smiling to myself I thought, *"People have their own idea or image of what they see or want to see."*

There came a turning point. It was during that time that I started writing this book. I remember writing a few pages at first, then a few chapters, not really knowing my purpose for the book. Slowly it all started to come together. One by one all my doubts began to fall to the floor as I saw the pages of my book taking form in front of me. I shouted to myself like I used to when I was a kid, "Duh, Astha! Why didn't you think of this earlier?" **"Your purpose is to share your awakening and experiences with others."** That was a realization. *Suddenly I knew I was very close to that moment when I would never again look back at my life with a single regret.*

As the messages came through me, I would open my laptop. **One by one the pages of this book came pouring out.** My spiritual journey evolved further through the process of writing. As I finished the first draft I started seeing and feeling connected to the bigger picture behind my own story. Then I remembered what people had told me about the process of writing and how it can be a great medium to use to sift through one's mind. *Writing can help a person come out of a difficult phase in life. It is cathartic.*

I began spending more time with my parents. The late-evening reality music show would draw me into their room where we would enjoy the rhythm and notes of the singers. *Music bridges generation gaps.* That phase of my life took a few years to settle.

Eventually I got my reason to go back to my work. A family friend from Los Angeles, whom I address as Ved Uncle, called on his next visit to Delhi. He was in the city for a few days on business and was staying at The Leela Palace Hotel in Chanakyapuri. He invited me to lunch. It was my first reason to escape from home. I told my mother and she allowed me to meet him. He and I spoke about many things over the meal. I tried to complain about my family but he said I should never feel badly about them as they are my biggest well-wishers. **He reminded me that there is a reason for everything and what was happening was preordained.** "Your parents have a point of view. They are parents. Let them do what they feel best. You dance. You have so much experience – you need to become a production manager," he said and added, "They will come around in time. In the meantime, do your work." I was happy to be away from home eating sushi with him. "Ok, but how?"

I asked. "I will help you," he said. A few years ago he had welcomed me to Los Angeles to present my Sufi performance at various events organized by him. He was an art lover and his family appreciated classical music. He also supported Indian artistes. We finished our meal and I left for home. The next day he called and asked for the details of my organization so that he could partially fund my production.

In the next week I made a quick visit to the Kamani Auditorium. I had an idea in my mind that I had begun developing. It was time to go on stage and use the might of my sword – my dance, my medium of expression – to portray my strength as an artiste. I arrived at the office. I signed in the register to confirm the staging of my show in the next year and made an initial payment towards the reservation of the hall.

That night I told my parents, "I'm presenting my first stage production at the Kamani." My mother immediately reacted, "How can you think of such a thing at this time?" "Mom, it's my work," I replied. "I need to raise funds to further my creative endeavours." "It's too far from home," she said, being her usual protective self. "It's not that easy, it's impractical," said my father. I just walked away from the dining table.

I started laying down ideas for the production. At the same time, I looked for a way out of my situation. I began jotting down a plan in my notebook. I realized: **artistes have a great responsibility in that they hold a community together with their expression. Their works represent the common voice. I needed to represent something powerful in my production.**

My family became good friends with some neighbours who lived down the block from our building, and all of us began spending our evenings together singing and dancing. Those were precious moments for my family.

Your family is a trigger to your personal growth. It is your responsibility to figure out your journey and to step into your lessons. That was one of my biggest learnings.

In those days my cousin from London happened to visit her parents in Gurugram and she came over to meet us. She could not believe what I had been through. She was very supportive and asked, "Astha, do you do any form of physical exercise other than dance? You must build your strength back. Get a personal trainer." She insisted that I exercise regularly for my own good. I was convinced. I found a trainer the same week.

It was summer and the pool became my best friend in the Delhi heat. I began spending the late afternoons swimming and, additionally, going to a gym for my workout. Or I would go jogging, either in the mornings or evenings. Through regular exercise I regained my inner and outer strength and was soon ready to go back to my studio to begin practicing for my production.

Why does one have to go through a difficult phase in life? ***It is because our soul needs to go through purification.*** *It is a process through which we may clearly see our own life's purpose & start walking towards it. As* The Bhagavad Gita *teaches: Take the correct action.*

"It is not between you and them. It is between you and your Higher Self."

In Search of Love: A Musical Production

"No one knew what lay within the folds of my heart, but this said it all."

Getting back to my work was a relief from all the challenges I was facing with my family. Once I was at my studio in Greater Kailash, I felt alive. I was working and doing what I love most. Ved Uncle had been right in suggesting that I create my own production with my years of experience as a performer.

My production was a themed ballet called *In Search of Love.* The title reflected my journey of coming to India and the state of bliss that I was looking for through my dance. The ballet was filled with poetry and music and had intricately-woven choreography.

I made my characters resemble some of those of my previous works who had inspired me. Two of them stood out: a palace courtesan who is abandoned by the prince whom she adores. She is in her room, heart-broken… Then she sets out to become a *jogan* – a seeker, who one day stumbles upon the meaning of love. The second was a traveller – a wanderlust, who discovers that each moment is eternal and that love is real.

I began jotting down notes on the palace courtesan – the central character. She was played by me. I imagined a transformation taking place in her, and that became the theme of the production. Soon I had an outline of the screenplay in front of me. It was unlike any other story I had read. As the title 'in search of love' suggests, it was not a love story like that of Mumtaz Mahal and Shah Jahan, but rather *it attempted to depict, through dance and music, the alchemy or mystical transformation brought about by the emotion of love.* I imagined the costumes, the dialogues, the dances and even the set. It was right there clear in my mind and imagination prior to our performance on stage. The characters, who were inspired by historical figures, were all tied together to the common theme of finding a deeper meaning to life through love. They went in and out of the narrative, all moving towards the same quest.

It took us months of practice at my studio. My team of dancers and eminent musicians became an intrinsic part of my journey. The production changed me and set me in a positive direction. It was more than just a theatrical dance show for me.

When I began working on the production, one day I waited for my designer, Devika, to come to my studio. I had met her in Lucknow through my association with Muzaffar Ali. She had agreed to handle the creative aspects of the production and arrived while I was getting ready in my room. My maid opened the door for her. By the time I came out she was already seated with a glass of water.

We started working on my laptop, pulling out my photographs from a recent photoshoot. She started selecting pictures for the brochure. "How about these?" she asked, as I put the selected pictures into a folder. I could hear my maid in the kitchen. "You must join me for lunch afterwards," I told her. Then we started discussing a design for the brochure. "Any idea where the person from the public relations agency has disappeared?" I asked. She shook her head to say no. "Take it easy. They're probably busy with another event," she replied. "I wonder why they aren't answering my calls," I said. "Anyway, they'll get back to you." She caught my frustration and suggested I try for another agency.

Apart from the nitty-gritty of the main production, there was a lot of work that took up my time and energy. I was scattered in many directions, so I immediately took up my designer's advice and called a friend who recommended a professional agency that handled the works of many artistes in Delhi. I called the agency, followed it up with a brief meeting at my studio, and then gave them the job of managing the publicity for the event.

Next came the music, lighting and set design. We created a unique introductory symphony of sarangis as the tabla complemented the rhythm of our turns and feet. The Khan Saabs, my musicians, arrived at my studio. "You are one hour late," I said. We sat down to play. When Amaan Ali started playing the tabla, my feet started moving automatically to the rhythm. Next, I changed the pattern with my feet. With a quick glance at my feet he caught the change which he translated on his tabla.

Devika came again the next week. “Take a look at these logo samples,” she said. I pointed to some options. She promised to send me the finished design by email the following day. The next morning when I opened my inbox, the logo was there. She designed all the brochures well in time. “Where are we on the posters?” she asked. “I’ll send you the photographs from the new shoot,” I said to her, making a mental note.

The new dancers, who had auditioned for the production, arrived at my studio. A few minutes later the rest of my dancers were there too, moving their feet.

I continued with the music sessions. “So where were we in the ghazal the last time?” I asked Amaan Ali. “At this wording,” he said. He started playing his tabla. When he stopped, Ahsan Ali started humming a tune. He paused and then started humming again. He pulled out his sarangi, adjusted the knobs and began playing the freshly composed ghazal “Uzr Aane mein…” As the notes flowed, I could imagine the court scene of the heartbreak the whole time.

“What next?” asked Ahsan Ali. “We have thought of a thumri,” said Amaan Ali and played the rhythm on his tabla. The music patterns came on perfectly. Suddenly I remembered, “What about the *tarana*?” referring to a type of composition based on Persian syllables. “Don’t worry dear,” said Ahsan Ali, “I’ll send it to you.” I nodded in agreement. The tea arrived as the musicians put away their instruments.

I sat with the agency team to discuss the possible strategies for the media coverage. We wanted the maximum amount of publicity for the event. And we had to hurry the work, for we were on a short deadline after hiring the new agency.

At the recording studio I had my headphones on as I listened to the music. “It sounds too much like the song in the movie,” I said. It had already been a few hours of recording. “It’s ok. It’s a classical composition and it can be done in any way.” My musicians tried to convince me. “Haven’t you heard it in the movie *Bajirao Mastani*?” said the sound engineer sarcastically from the back. I looked at him. The large set in the Hindi movie flashed in front of my eyes as I remembered the dancers entering on the same song, “Albela sajan aayo ri…” “How do you think the music director of the movie got it?” asked one of the Khan Saabs, “obviously from the original classical piece.”

We finished the composition after lunch. “Shall we break for today?” asked Ahsan Ali. I looked at the clock and thought how quickly six hours had gone by. “Sure. So when can we meet and finish the recording?” I asked, “the show is only weeks away?” “Next weekend,” he assured me. The musicians left except for Amaan Ali who was still packing up. “Next time let’s set all our Kathak bols for the piece before the recording so we can just lay them one by one on the music track,” came his voice. Then I started, *Dhatita dha dha tita...* We both finished the notations at the same time. We added one more bol to our final list and called it a day.

As we walked out of the studio, I remembered my long sequence with the dancers and the steps I had created in my mind. I waited for Amaan Ali to carry his bags to his car and bade him farewell. As my driver turned the car around towards the highway, I went over the entire theme in my mind. Was I missing anything? The sound, the visuals, the lighting, ah!

I remembered I needed to call a set designer. We turned the corner to Greater Kailash and arrived home.

The next day, my first batch of dancers arrived in the studio: Pallavi, Sanskriti, Deepak, Richa, Henna and Mayukh. I placed them in their positions in a diagonal line and began the choreography. After noon, the second batch of dancers joined us and we went over everything we had done. I heard one of my girls discussing a particular movement while I was explaining the sequence. I looked at her and told her to stop conversing with the other girls, "Focus on your own posture and correction." We started over and did the entire piece without any further distraction. In the next week Shivam, a choreographer I had called, came in to teach the contemporary dance movements in the production. He also offered to record short profiles of the artistes before the event.

I was rehearsing with my dancers. Sweat dripped from my forehead as the lilting sound of the sarangi carried me through my turns. They continued rehearsing the piece as I began making a video film. I looked at the girls. "Sit down on this count." I had said it nearly ten times. I saw a girl bending down to fasten her ghungroos yet again. It was the last straw. I stopped recording, took my bag and stormed off. "Didi, please come back!" My oldest dancer who had been with me the longest, rushed after me to take me back into the studio. I took a deep breath and started the recording all over again.

The designer finalized the posters and brochures for the mega event and they were ready for printing. At the recording studio the next week, I was overwhelmed by all that was going on around me. Ved Uncle sensed my emotions on the phone. "Sometimes things are not entirely in our control, right?"

he said, trying to encourage me. That week, as we finished the recording of the music, I felt better. The wind hit our faces as we walked out on the main road, past all the cars in the parking lot. "See you at the Kamani Auditorium," I said to my musicians with a smile.

The day before the show, at the stage and technical rehearsal, there was excitement in the air. I caught a few procrastinators amongst the dancers and moved them out to a side so they could not copy the steps of the others. They had not been consistent in their practice and it was affecting everybody in the group. They were not happy with the shifting of their positions but had to cooperate with me. Suddenly I had their full attention and a renewed sense of participation.

The show, a grand success, was held at the Kamani Auditorium in September 2018. The countdown started two weeks before the date with the media sending out daily notices in the popular newspapers of Delhi and the National Capital Region to announce the show. They carried several full-page features in the papers on the techniques we had used to create the production. I was happy that my brainchild *In Search of Love* had been well received. I had always envisioned it in that way – to be staged at the Kamani on a large scale. To me it embodied, in itself, a distinctive style of ballet reflective of the North Indian tradition of devotion called *bhakti.*

During the show, the first hour went by in pin-drop silence in the auditorium. The thematic dance, set in chemistry to the music in the classical tradition, gradually transitioned to a modern-day version of the wanderlust. It had the audience clapping along with the beats. At the curtain call, we bowed together to a thundering ovation.

I received the applause of the audience and spoke about each of my artistes.

The production was my labour of love. It was a comprehensive process of hard work and dedication that made it joyous and self-rewarding. And just as it had been multiple times before my own production – it was about creating with others, a sense of unity, rhythmic compositions and devotion on stage. The process was unique and enjoyable. No words can fully explain those deep moments of melodic transformation and the satisfaction of working together with a team.

At the culmination of the project, things started to change. I got much appreciation as a choreographer, dancer and storyteller. **You must learn to appreciate yourself by channeling your efforts into the right direction. Do not be limited by your circumstances. Step forth in your own light, do your best – you will rise and the world will recognize you.**

Many people ask me, "Was the production really your journey?" "It definitely reflected my personal transformation," is my answer.

I chose dance as my spiritual path. *I believe that when we get on stage, we become vehicles for the divine to speak through, and we let the audience connect and be inspired in their own way.* I hear Osho's voice speaking within me: "Be totally in it. Let the dancer become the dance." Due to my passion and my commitment to dance, every time I prepare for a show, tears roll down my face instinctively as I feel myself merging into the part that I am to embody on stage. Every time I get up to dance, I hear the music reverberating in my mind as I become a vehicle for the divine. And those watching the dance enjoy it as much.

“**When every cell of the body is involved in what one does, time disappears. Dance became that to me.** And that is the meaning of the word ‘wanderlust’ in the production because it is known that, “Not all who wander are lost.” **The theme depicts love is a state within yourself. Love is a state defined within you.** Despite all the challenges in staging such a production, I had done it!

Friends and Touring in America

"Humans seek material pleasures in life, but real wealth is in finding your own inner happiness."

My career during my years in India required my sincerity and devotion to my art, to myself and to others. That was it. I was not required to think of anything else. *It was what life demanded of me during those years.*

One day I woke up with a recollection of my days growing up in Los Angeles and I wondered about my old pals. "Where are all of them?" I said to myself. I called Vicky, and when he picked up the phone he was amazed to hear my voice. "So you miss those good old days… well, you pretty much sound the same," he said. I was relieved at the reassurance that nothing much had changed.

A few days later, out of the blue, I called Nina, my old college-dormitory best friend. We had had a long gap of silence after I moved. She did not answer my call so I left a message, "What's up? Long time!" Then a long paragraph about how life in India had bogged me down. Her usual friendly response was, "Well, come back to the US!"

Life had certainly not gone the way I had expected. I had always been optimistic after my move. However, I longed to live my own life again the way it used to be. And that is when I began to think about the possibility of returning to America.

One day Meera called to say she was visiting Delhi. She landed at the airport around midnight and texted me. I woke up when the doorbell rang. She walked into my house at 3 am with a big bag behind her. She looked at me with her soft eyes and we hugged. We sat up all night talking. She understood what I had been through. The next day I took her to buy fabric, lace and embellishments for her dance costumes. A full day of bargaining and we were exhausted.

It was as if time had never passed. We recalled the way we used to roam around in the United States, sometimes shopping, sometimes dancing, and once in a while hanging out during late nights after our shows. Ah! That connection! That was what I had missed through the years. I expressed it to her.

Meera went to Goa for some weeks while I got busy preparing for a Tamil television festival in Chennai. The Chennaivuyyal Festival featured several dancers from different parts of India. Meera flew down to Chennai to be with me for a few more days.

The day after the show, Churchill Pandian, Meera and I drove to Mahabalipuram to take a look at the beautiful temple sculptures in daylight. Along the way we stopped at roadside shops for their display of different artefacts. A striking display of old wooden doors, in particular, caught our attention.

In Mahabalipuram, we enjoyed ourselves dancing and taking photographs near the carved pillars of the cave temples.

We drove to the rocky beach of the Shore Temple just as the sun set. The waves were crashing as it was high tide and Meera excitedly stood by the water in various dance poses. I laughed and clicked pictures as a crescent moon shown from behind some clouds in the dark sky. Then I took a pose. Finally, she took my hand and led me back to where Mr Pandian was waiting for us. Such bonds of dance and togetherness are rare and everlasting.

In 2019, I got a call from Mr Pandian for a performance in the United States for a stage show titled *Ganga to Kaveri*. My mother agreed to my going because of her trust in Churchill Pandian. She considered him a serious cultural entrepreneur who was promoting the dance style of Kathak in India. Mr Pandian and I started planning the trip. When we were arranging for our tickets, Ratna Kumar, a renowned Bharatanatyam dance exponent from Texas, got in touch with Mr Pandian. She offered to collaborate with him on the show and requested him to finalize all the names of the dancers. The concert was to be held at the Midtown Arts & Theater Center Houston (MATCH) in Texas, and in the trip we also included workshops at various dance schools in San Diego and Chicago. It was the perfect timing of summer to be touring the States. I quickly called Nina once the show was confirmed. "You're really coming to Texas?" she asked excitedly. She had happily settled down many years ago in Texas with her husband and two children.

After a brief visit to Los Angeles to see my friends, I arrived at the Houston airport. I was picked up by Mr Pandian and Ratna Kumar, and we drove to the latter's academy.

It was a prestigious location. The walls of Ratna Kumar's dance school were adorned with framed awards and photographs of her and her students. We held our rehearsal for the show while her students watched us enthusiastically. Later, Nina came to the academy to pick me up and take me to her house in Sugarland.

She pulled the car up by the side of her large pool. "Home sweet home!" she exclaimed. I walked into her living room in her dream house and of course her dream life. Her children came running down the stairs from their rooms and started playing with me until Nina came in to send them back up to finish their homework. "So?" she said, "now that you're an Indian star and you've lived your dreams, how do you feel being back here after so long?" When I sat with her and shared my story, she listened with a sympathetic ear. We talked about my tours. She also agreed that it takes parents time to understand their children sometimes. She said, "You took the step to move to India because of your talent and to be with them. There is no turning back for you now, is there?" I completely agreed. After dinner she put her children to bed, then we stayed up for some time talking before I wished Nina and her husband a good night. "I better hit the sack otherwise I won't to be able to perform tomorrow, dude," I said to her husband, enjoying my simple slang again and letting loose with my old friends. I remembered their wedding in Toronto where I had danced and also given a long speech amidst all our friends and family members. I had always been more like a sister to her.

The next day I performed at the MATCH Auditorium in Houston. My friends and the organizers were proud of me, seeing me in my chosen form performing on stage. The rest of the month flew by meeting wonderful friends and colleagues and also building more memories before and after each show.

The day I landed in Delhi, my mother was at the airport. A thick layer of pollution and dust gathered around me. I sat in the car feeling no relief of coming back. "Why don't you try settling down in the US?" she read my mind. We went back home to Gurugram. *As I thought of going back to the United States and making my plans around it, I actually started feeling happy once again.*

"Life works in curious ways. Sometimes we do not have the answers to our questions, but something comes along and shows us the way."

Back to Cali

"Let your spirit shine through your actions."

I realized that I needed to make a decision about moving back to California or 'Cali'. I thought of opening a dance academy on the West Coast where I used to live. As a call for students, I began posting notices on social media about my new academy. The response I got convinced me of my decision. My parents accepted that I wanted to go back to America.

My mother's friend who lives in Ventura County in California, saw my notices and called me. The first thing she said was, "I heard you came to Los Angeles recently, and you didn't call me?" "Uh uh aunty, I had tours and barely had any time during my last trip." I tried to look for more excuses. "It's ok," she said, "I saw your notice about opening your school here in LA." "Yes, aunty," I said. She offered, "I'm so happy! You know, LA needs good Kathak teachers like you. If you want I can recommend your name in some of the community centres here and let's see what they say." "Sure aunty," I replied.

She was keen on dance herself and had choreographed the entire dance routine for the Vishwa Hindu Parishad function in Torrance during my school days. "Ek Radha... Ek Meera… dono ne…" the steps of the dance were still vivid in my mind. I could see her standing as I sat on the stage next to her, pretending as if I had a small one-stringed instrument in my hands. She had shown me how to hold it and how to gracefully sit down with it as part of my dance. After that, she had danced around me.

After my conversation with my aunt, my mother was also very happy. She really liked her and they had been close in the earlier days. "Oh, you'll be just like the other teachers in the area. They're all very well established." My mother repeated the lines my aunt had said on the phone. "But you must be exclusive and offer students the real value of our culture," was the additional advice my aunt had given. "Come and stay here for six months and see how you feel," she had suggested.

Los Angeles, lined with palm trees along the ocean side, welcomed me with its fresh breeze. People walking by were friendly and efficient and I was glad to be back here. The work ethics were – what you give is what you get. Hard work led to results in one's career and personal life. Value for time was an important building block of society, it could not be undermined. And nor could the outgoing personality that everyone donned. In fact, it was suave and smart to be friendly and respect time.

My sister-in-law picked me up from the airport. We stopped for lunch and then she dropped me off at a mobile phone shop from where I could get my new cellphone number. Giggling as I looked past all the familiar area codes on the West Coast, I selected a number for myself that would be easy to remember.

I then proceeded to rent a car and drove to the accommodation that I had taken. On the way, I listened to rap songs on Kiss FM, my favorite hip hop music radio station since my days in high school and college. I was surprised I still remembered the lyrics of the songs. I arrived at the house before 7:30 pm – the exact time given to my landlady. She opened the door, showed me my room and handed me my set of keys. And then I sat down with her to enjoy the dinner she had prepared.

The next morning I visited my bank and after lunch drove to my first dance class. I had enrolled some students before I arrived in the States. It was also arranged with some temples that I would perform in their precincts during the Hindu cultural celebrations. Shortly afterwards, I started teaching at the temples as well as at community centres.

On Friday mornings I would drive north up to Ventura for one of my sets of students and spend the weekend with my aunt. On Saturday mornings we would drive to Kings County, to a Hindu temple. The students would be eagerly waiting with their ghungroos on. Each student would usually be accompanied by a family member. Many of them would come from far – some travelling an hour on the highway. The parents were keen to expose their children to Indian culture with the right teacher. They would watch as I went around instructing and adjusting the hand movements. “Keep your torso straight,” I said to one of the girls as I moved her arms upwards. I adjusted her hands and moved on. The students usually watched each other and corrected themselves quickly. At my aunt’s home, she and I would watch movies and share stories about India. Time on the weekends just flew by. On weekdays I had other batches of students in my area and more towards the canyons.

Driving around in Los Angeles was just as I remembered it from the past. I still had memories of the same grocery store in the neighborhood, the same jogging pathway by the beach, and my high school name on a billboard as I drove past it every day. When other family friends started finding out I was in the area, they began inviting me to their homes. Seeing the same faces that I had grown up with had something so familiar to it – I remembered the family group in which I was raised and the fun we used to have. I felt at home because of the warmth and support they offered me.

I started driving every morning to the beach. While jogging I would see people running or walking their dogs. Sometimes a poodle would come up to me and sniff my shoes; sometimes it would be a breed that I did not know. They were well groomed and looked cute. The owners were cheerful, polite and well-mannered.

"Damn! Why can't it always be this good?" I said to myself out loud as I ran back to where I was parked. I knew I was close to my parking meter running out. I took in another few deep inhalations of the cool ocean breeze. Most people think money or power alone can give them joy and happiness. I used to feel the same. **But now I realize that even freedom and joy in life have to be earned.** Just like that ocean breeze that blew the hair on my face away. When I got into my car, the meter time had nearly finished. Just in time, I thought as I turned on the ignition. Soon I was zipping past the few cars on the Pacific Coast Highway with the ocean right next to me. My hands reached for the volume on the stereo playing Kiss FM. I could see a clear, bright and sparkling line below the horizon. **This should be**

everyone's dream, I laughed out loud to myself. I pulled up at the front porch of my accommodation where I took my shoes off and went inside.

On one weekend between my classes, I drove on the highway leading to the canyons and further up to a quiet retreat in the mountains. There my friend Isaah was attending a class of African dance being held in a yoga studio. He was doing a jive with other students and we waved at each other through the thin glass windows of the studio as I stood outside near my parked car. He smiled and gestured that he would join me soon. We were meeting after a long time.

After his class we talked non-stop and then drove up a series of winding roads to his house. When I went inside, I looked around at the same place where I had spent time before. "Ohmigod!" I said, "the house feels different, *but you my friend have not changed one bit!*" His presence always seemed to have a profound influence on me and my journey.

"How is life now, now that you're back in LA?" he asked curiously as I sipped my tea slowly. I spoke as he was one of those few that I could talk with. Seeing the look of contentment on my face that explained everything anyway, he said that I looked happy.

I took a deep breath when we stepped outside into his picturesque garden. His house was surrounded by clouds. The air was fresh, crisp and clean. The canyons in Los Angeles were even more peaceful than I remembered. Breathing deeply, I had a good look around, ready to leave. "See ya," I said, looking back and murmuring something to his cats as I walked to my car.

During the drive back home at night through the canyons, it felt like eternity. Stars shone perfectly in the dark sky. Not a speck of particle was out of place. The cold air hit my face as I zipped past the endless canyons winding around each other. My car went past the last canyon as I entered the highway. It was good to be back.

I had come a long way on my journey. What was different in me? Was there something different in me now? Had I discovered it? Had I overcome my biggest challenge? Self-doubt? Misery? He had seen it in me and my look of confidence. It was true what he had said, *"We are a part of a larger flow of evolution. We are here to do something. And if we are true to that purpose, we'll help humanity towards a higher purpose."* It felt like an eternal moment. *One journey had come to an end. Another was waiting to begin.*

Life in the United States at that time revolved around the belief that – your career can lead to success and success can be your key to true freedom. However, freedom can be defined by so many things and in so many ways. It is an experience that is different for each individual.

To complement my lifestyle, I joined a fun and exciting fitness programme at a gym led by young fitness freaks that made exercise enjoyable. It was probably not a coincidence that they were all alumni of my high school which was just up the street. It was probably also not a coincidence that I had chosen that area to live in.

I believe: **The greatest freedom is achieved within ourselves. True freedom comes from self-knowing.**

Journey from Beyond

"I would not be where I am today if I had followed someone else's path."

I had to return to Delhi for rehearsals for a tour in Saudi Arabia with the Caracalla dance company. My mother opened the door when I arrived from the airport. As we sat down, my parents were full of praise for all that I had done by myself in such a short time in Los Angeles. We reminisced about our past as I told them about my new experiences that brought back many good memories of my brother and me growing up. A sense of love and belonging engulfed the family in that moment. The issues we had between us were left in the past, and as the days progressed, all our troubles seemed far behind. *It felt so good to be home.*

Shortly after that, the Coronavirus pandemic period started. On my way back to India from the Middle East in March 2020, I was detained at the Beirut airport for more than twenty-four hours. Even though I held an Overseas Citizenship of India (OCI) card, I was unsure whether I would be allowed to enter India easily or have to go through strict quarantine rules at the Delhi airport. I decided to take a flight from Beirut to London instead and spend time at my cousin sister's house in the suburbs.

I spent six months in and around the countryside of London. I engaged myself in finding new ways to present my dance that I was teaching online, learning new culinary skills and filling my leisure time taking walks in the parks. When I finally arrived in India once the lockdown was partially lifted, I continued to spend my time at home building my website and teaching on Zoom. Alongside, I also maintained a blog and wrote articles. One of my articles that was published in a newspaper talks about certain issues that India has been facing from the last century.

The pandemic went on. It made many people realize what their real needs in life are and to never feel a lack about what they do not have. If we have a roof over our heads, food on our tables – what else do we need other than our close companions in life? The pandemic was an eye-opener.

The title of this book, ***Door to Heaven***, suggests a dancer's journey through struggles in her life to find the doorway to bliss or heaven. *The struggle is immaterial for a seeker as it is the means to an end.* My quest was not for material gain. It was an evolution process through various milestones. A life of growth and self-evaluation at every step is not a course that everyone takes. **Eventually, enlightenment is that doorway that a person seeks on the spiritual path.**

This book is about my journey from Los Angeles to India and the time I spent as a dancer discovering my own inner purpose, dreams and goals. **My devotion to my art aligned me**

with my own quest as a spiritual seeker, and I am grateful for all the lessons that I learnt along the way.

I have visited many countries to share my culture and have created a niche for myself in the world. My academy is to further all that I have stood for over the years.

Life is eternal. It is viewed as a process of birth and death. We shed our bodies and are born again. Like this we go on through cycles of births and deaths. *We go through many lives struggling to learn our lessons. What is the point of our coming back for so many lifetimes?*

To appreciate our gifts and talents and to use these to serve our higher purpose. Our purpose is that with which we align the most in our lives. We come back to value each other, grow together, and to build a time on earth together of peace and harmony. Our purpose is also to realize our true nature – which is God.

Life is a purifying process. We are here to purify our soul. Our soul never dies. Life leads us up to that *doorway to heaven* and it is up to us to realize our true nature which is eternal.

Time on earth can be spent in ignorance like the passing of a dream. We can either just sleep through our entire lives or we can take the opportunity to awaken to our true purpose. ***And one life spent in awareness of a higher purpose is enough to awaken to our true nature.*** I am here to contribute towards making the world a better place to live in, in my own way.

When I began writing this book, I used to read a lot from the library of contemporary spiritual authors. Many of those writings continue to inspire me. Messages to lead us can come from various sources: through books, movies and even documentaries. *We each absorb various teachings depending upon our own lessons to be learnt.*

As one journey takes off, another one begins alongside the course and merges in. We can live many journeys in one lifetime. *I now felt ready to share my life with another person.*

I met an architect from Central Florida who contacted me over the phone while I was in India. Initially we spoke briefly, but as we exchanged more about our lives, we realized what a connection we had.

I flew down to be with him and his family in Florida, which is also known as The Sunshine State. Other than having a lot of similarities including our healthy lifestyles, he and I are like-minded and share many common interests.

To make a long story short, we got married within a couple of months with various events being held in both countries to build precious memories with all our loved ones. We now look forward to a fulfilling future together.

I remember the moment when he proposed to me on that day while we were checking out at a store. "I think we both agree we make a good couple?" he said. It was understood. All the lessons that I have shared in this book added up to that moment.

We went to picturesque monuments to shoot for my first production as a director/ choreographer.

In Search of Love official poster. A night to be remembered.

What is love? This musical explores the intense emotion

Dancer Astha Dixit; and (below) with her troupe

Looking out for the true meaning of love

A superlative performer and an artist of great calibre, Astha, has performed in innumerable international festivals

SYEDA EBA

Raised in the United States, Astha Dixit - an engineer by profession - always knew that she was meant to dance. So, to continue her Kathak training, Dixit quit a lucrative career and chose to return back to India.

"As a child, I learned the basics of Kathak in Los Angeles. But with increasing responsibilities and busy schedule, it was hard to pursue my passion. I took admission in engineering and went on to work in the same field for two consecutive years. But realizing that I was born to be a dancer, I moved to India and started my training with guru Harish Gangani and Malti Shyam," stated Astha.

A superlative performer and an artist of great calibre, Astha has performed in many top festivals including the ones held in Muscat, Oman, Kuwait, Bahrain, and also at the world famous Baalbeck International festival in Lebanon. She has been a regular performer at Jahan-e-Khusrau every year for Muzaffar Ali.

Thrilled to represent India on the international stage, Astha feels Kathak as a dance form still needs a lot of exposure.

"There is a lot that we need to do to popularize this dance form. It's sad that people still are unaware of Kathak in various parts of the world. I remember, when I performed in Baalbeck, it was the first time that people over there were introduced to Kathak. For the first time, they heard the sound of ghunghroos which left them mesmerized," mentioned Astha who gets her inspiration from within.

It is her delicate art of abhinaya and natural expression on Sufi Kalaams that touch people's heart. One such performance, where she unraveled the mysteries of love, was held in Kamani auditorium, New Delhi, on September 7.

Titled 'In search of love', the Sufi musical was based on her journey and discoveries as a dancer, as well as her intense work on Sufi poetries. Soothing music synced with beautiful expressions and graceful gestures, the performance as a whole was a treat to watch. The main direction and choreography was by Astha Dixit whereas contemporary choreography was done by Shivam Chauhan. Music composers Ahsan Ali and Amaan Ali struck a melodious chord to make the production a complete masterpiece.

Explaining Kathak is a form of story telling, Astha said, "A dancer uses her body as a vehicle to tell stories. In fact, the word Kathak is derived from 'Katha' - meaning story. In the ancient days, the Kathakars were story tellers who used to go from village to village narrating stories in an artistic manner."

I was so happy to get amazing groundbreaking reviews in leading newspapers and journals of India.

In the US with Churchill Pandian and an accomplished set of classical dancers.

Always creating new dance pieces for live audiences.

With my musicians. We call ourselves 'Meraaj Collective'.

www.ingramcontent.com/pod-product-compliance
Ingram Content Group UK Ltd.
Pitfield, Milton Keynes, MK11 3LW, UK
UKHW041629190726
13854UKWH00006B/2387

9 789393 029478